Blessings & Emp~
Dr. Gwyneth
&
ambassador
Star
John 14:12

Blessings & Empowerment

Dr. Ruth

Ambassador
Kim

John 14:19

Azusa Street Outpouring
Unleashing the Holy Spirit,

Then and Now

Dr. Gwyneth Williams & Star Williams
with Bishop Otis G. Clark

AZUSA STREET OUTPOURING
Unleashing the Holy Spirit, Then and Now

©1993, 2011, 2018 Dr. Gwyneth Williams & Star Williams. All right reserved.

No part of this book may be reproduced, distributed, stored in a retrieval system, or transmitted in any form or by any means, including photocopying, recording, or other electronic or mechanical methods, without the prior written permission of the author.

For permission request, right to the author & publisher, addressed Attention: Permissions Coordinator at the address below:

Author & Publisher Contact:
Life Enrichment Publishing
www.lemglobal.org
Office: +1-918-288-0400
WhatsApp: +1-918-409-7700
admin@lemglobal.org

ISBN: 978-1-949594-02-7

THIRD EDITION

First Edition 1993, Second Edition 2011, Third Edition Published 2018

- First published in 1993 as "The Azusa Mission" by Life Enrichment Ministries with a Holiness Mission. Authors: Bishop Otis Clark and Dr. Gwyneth Williams
- "The Azusa Outpouring: Unleashing the Holy Spirit, Signs, Wonders and Miracles" was re-published by AuthorHouse 4/29/2011 Authors: Bishop Otis Clark and Dr. Gwyneth Williams
- This is the 3rd Revised and Updated Edition, "Azusa Street Outpouring: Unleashing the Holy Spirit, Then and Now" Authors: Dr. Gwyneth Williams and Star Williams with Bishop Otis G. Clark

Ordering information: Quantity sales. Special discounts are available for quantity purchases by corporations, associations, and others. For details contact the author & publisher at the address above. Orders by US trade bookstores and wholesalers. Please contact the same.

Because of the dynamic nature of the Internet, and Web addresses or links contained in this book may have changed since publication and may no longer be valid.

Printed in the United States of America

Table of Contents

FORWARD..11
PREFACE...13
INTRODUCTION..17
Chapter 1: THE HOLINESS MOVEMENT......................................19
    Contributions to The Movement..19
    Holiness Movement's Effects on Denominations...................20
    The Holiness Church and Its Theology................................20
    W.H. Durham's Theology..21

Chapter 2: THE PENTECOSTAL REVIVAL...................................23
    Charles Parham..23
    Parham and the Pentecostal Movement................................24
    Speaking in Glossolalia..25
    Twentieth Century Accounts of Glossolalia.........................27

Chapter 3: WILLIAM J. SEYMOUR..29
    Seymour's Life..29
    Seymour and Parham..30
    Seymour and Julia Hutchison..32
    Seymour and Edward S. Lee...33
    Bonnie Brae Street..35
    California Meetings...36
    Renovation of Azusa..38
    Seymour Makes Request for Credentials.............................39
    Seymour Speaks in Glossolalia..39
    Seymour's Preaching Style and Order of Service..................39
    Seymour Marries and Conflict Arises..................................41
    Seymour the Central Figure...43

Chapter 4: TESTIMONIES OF AZUSA 45
    J. Roswell Flower...47
    T.B. Barrett..47
    Emma Cotton Mother of Azusa...49
    Did Azusa Fail? 51
    Azusa Spreading Abroad: Ministers and Workers
    from Distant Lands...51
    The Purchase of The Azusa Mission..................................53
    Pentecost in San Francisco...53
    Andrew H. Argues' Letter to Azusa..................................53
    Charles H. Mason Receives Baptism at Azusa....................55

Chapter 5: NEWSPAPER REPORTS..59
    Apostolic Faith Newspaper...59
    L.A. Times Report..59
    Reports of Seymour and Parham.......................................60
    The Wave Swept the World..61

Chapter 6: AZUSA WORSHIPERS..65
    Frank Bartleman...65
    The Armenians...69

Chapter 7: VIEWS ABOUT TONGUES AND THE HOLY SPIRIT........71
    The Holy Spirit..72
    Jesus and the Holy Spirit..76
    Jesus' Emphasis on the Work of the Holy Spirit................77
    Azusa and the Holy Spirit...77
    Tongues and Interpretation...78
    Have Gifts Ceased? 79
    Organizational Lines..83
    Pentecostal Churches...85

  Christianity Today..93

Chapter 8: THE CHARISMATIC AND PENTECOSTAL
  CHURCH TODAY..95
  Results of the Pentecostal and Charismatic Movements...........96
  Moving With the Spirit...98
  The Next Generation..99
  The 100 Year Prophecy..99

Chapter 9: AZUSA NOW..101
  China 1986..101
  Testimonies in China..104
  Bahamas, Andros Island 1987 and 1989.............................106
  Jamaica 1990, 1993 and 2010..109
  Mexico 1990, and 2000...110
  England 1987, 1988, 1998, 2011, 2014 and 2015...................111
  France 1987, 1988, and 2015..112
  Zimbabwe, Africa 2006 and 2007......................................112
  Bishop Otis Clark..114
  Dad is a World Traveler...115
  Canada 2008, 2010 and 2012..122
  Azusa Now 2013-2015..125
  Azusa Now Haiti and Colombia July 2013 Mission................126
  Cali, Colombia Azusa Now..127
  Haiti Azusa Now...129
  Haiti Testimonies..131
  Azusa Now Anniversary..133
  Brazil Azusa Now...133
  Asia Azusa Now...135
  Continuing the Legacy 2017-2018.....................................140

Highlighted Testimonies..141
Prophetic Mapping...143
Unity Prayer Quilt...144
Azusa Lamp...146
Supernatural Provision..149
School Outreaches...149
Pentecost and Passover..151

Chapter 10: SIGNS, WONDERS AND THE ANOINTING................ 153
Signs and Wonders..153
The Anointing...156
What is the Anointing...157
Supernatural Strength..158
Manifestations of the Blessing..................................159
The Cost of the Anointing..162
The Quenching Agents...163
Remaining in the Spirit...167
Oiled Up..168
Jehovah El Shaddai...169
Mending Christ's Body..170
Reconciliation...173
Forgiveness..176
Righteousness Exalts..179

THE GREATEST MIRACLE...183
OTHER BOOKS AND STUDY COURSES...................................184
GLOBAL MINISTRY..185
MINISTERIAL ASSOCIATION...188
SCHOOL OF MISSIONS AND THEOLOGY...............................191
PARTNERSHIP..194

ABOUT THE AUTHORS 195
    Bishop Otis G. Clark: "Azusa Street Direct Link"................ 195
    Dr. Gwyneth Williams... 198
    Ambassador Star Williams.. 200

BIBLIOGRAPHY 203
ENDNOTES.. 207

Foreword

The Kingdom of God has been the talk of the world since John the Baptist arrived on the scene to prepare the way for the Messiah. After the baptism of Christ, Jesus continued the message of John: "Repent for the Kingdom of Heaven is near." Moves of God throughout history have begun with this message.

Jesus taught His disciples to pray, "Thy kingdom come, thy will be done on earth as it is in heaven." Whatever occurs on earth happens as a result of prayer and takes place in heaven first. Heaven wants revival; heaven desires miracles, and we are the vehicles through which His Spirit works. It is going to take people who carry great vision and passion for us to establish kingdom power and authority in our generation.

The power and purpose of God has never changed, nor has His strength weakened. Every generation has relied on men and women of God to make visible the invisible presence of God through signs, wonders, and miracles. The same Spirit that raised Christ from the dead is awaiting vessels (people) who will represent His cause to a searching world.

We have to go no further than our backyards to find a field awaiting harvest. The marketplace is clamoring for success with meaning—eternal meaning. Neighborhoods are flourishing with young minds looking for leadership, and nations are longing for a message of hope. This is our generation, and the command to "go" remains the same. We go in the name that is above all names, Jesus.

The foundation for all that we do must be love. The apostle Paul admonishes us by saying, "For in Christ Jesus neither circumcision nor uncircumcision has any value. The only thing that counts is faith expressing itself through love" (Galatians 5:6 NIV). Let our expression and our message be saturated with love. "Love covers over a multitude of sins" (1 Peter 4:8b NIV). "Love never fails" (1 Corinthians 13:8a NIV).

There are no obstacles greater than our God. There is nothing impossible to those who believe. As Patrick Snow once said, "Only those who can see the invisible can accomplish the impossible!" So, let's see it. As you read Dr. Williams and Bishop Clark's book, my prayer is that you will hear the sounds of revival in your life and in your land. Begin to press in and embrace your role in God's outpouring for our generation.

Dr. Williams and Bishop Clark have traveled the globe and gleaned a variety of experiences—as well as degrees—to tie together the work of the Spirit, the history of revival, and the Kingdom of God. They love God, the local church, and the nations of the earth. Their insights help give us a look into moves of God from different dispensations. Revival doesn't have to be a dream—it can be a reality. Let her heart for Holy Spirit fire get in you as you read their work.

Preface

Bishop Otis G. Clark had the prestigious opportunity to enter the great building on Azusa Street that held the greatest revival of modern times. He had a supernatural experience with God while in Los Angeles, an open vision that took him to heaven. Later he was mentored by the Azusa Street saints, specifically Mother Emma Cotton, he went into the Azusa Street Mission and was given the Power-of –Attorney by Bishop Driscoll, William J. Seymour's successor. Clark thanks God for Jesus Christ, God's son, and our Lord and Savior. The Lord allowed him to live for one-hundred and nine years telling about the importance of power of the Holy Spirit. Clark passed on the Power-of-Attorney for the Azusa Street ordination, impartation to his daughter and granddaughter on an Easter Sunday, April 16, 2006. During a significant time, the anniversary of Azusa and Passover.

THE ABOVE LETTER STATES "THIS INTRODUCES ELDER O. G. CLARK WHO HAS FULL POWER OF ATTORNEY TO DISCUSS ANY BUSINESS AS ABOVE. 'BISHOP DRISCOLL'"

Azusa Mission Power-of-Attorney Document given to Bishop Otis Clark

Clark greatest desire was to see the church world walk in Apostle Paul's teaching. He believed Paul's teachings will cause the churches to be winners and not losers in this present day. God's Church is the only hope. As the Apostle Paul has said, "Awake thou that sleepest and arise from the dead and Christ shall give thee light."

During this time, we must remember the blessing that God gave to His people at Azusa. This Pentecostal outpouring has affected the entire world, with over a billion proclaimed Pentecostals. Since 1906 the church has been affected by the outpouring at the Azusa Street Mission. God's message through the movement was that the church needed to accept the gifts of the Holy Spirit. "In 2011, a Pew Forum study of global Christianity found that there were an estimated 279 million classical Pentecostals, making 4 percent of the total world population and 12.8 percent of the world's Christian population Pentecostal."

The church today must continue in the teachings of Jesus by letting the Holy Spirit lead and guide us into all spiritual truths. When the church opens fully and humbles herself, as Seymour did when he prayed from behind two shoe boxes, then God can bring forth an awakening like the world has never known. If we humble ourselves, pray, and seek His face, God promises us that He will hear our prayers and heal our land.

It was humility, prayer and unity that caused the great revival of 1906. Those who first sought the Holy Spirit were in prayer when they received Him and were used as instruments to change the world. The Holy Spirit fell so powerfully on Azusa Street that people came from all over the world to see this great phenomenon that they heard about. People came from many livelihoods, every continent and every race. It was like the day of Pentecost in the Bible. God can and will do it again through us!

The purpose for this book is to give the reader some historical, theological, and practical insight of what happened at Azusa and what's happening present time. The contents will also reflect the great ripple effects that the Azusa movement had upon the Christian world. It has been celebrated as the wave continues to rise and as the power of God still works today through His Church.

For the Third Great Awakening,

Bishop Otis G. Clark & Dr. Gwyneth Williams

Introduction

The roots of the modern-day outpouring of the Spirit can be traced to a clapboard building during the turn-of-the-century in Los Angeles, California, Bishop Otis G. Clark became acquainted with Emma Mother of Azusa and Henry Cotton and lived in their home. Clark arrived in Los Angeles in 1921 after the Tulsa, Oklahoma race riot. Mother Emma Cotton mentored Clark. He was her personal driver, while Henry her husband was a porter on the train going from city to city. They tried to keep the Azusa churches open. They visited churches in California and other states where Azusa churches started.

In 1922 Seymour became ill and went to heaven. The revival that took place at the Azusa Street mission from 1906 to 1919 sparked the remarkable worldwide growth of the Pentecostal movement and its sister, the Charismatic renewal. Although this revival is significant for several reasons, Williams believes the most important lesson of Azusa Street for this current generation is the power of spiritual unity.

At Azusa, the long services were punctuated by fiery preaching, spontaneous singing and fervent praying. People were baptized with the Spirit, spoke in tongues, and fell under the power.

Led by William J. Seymour, a Black Holiness preacher, Azusa attracted people of all colors and all walks of life. Whites, Blacks, Hispanics, and Asians together experienced the Spirit's manifest presence. Seymour, who had received teaching on the Holy Spirit while listening through the doorway of an all-white classroom, knew his experience was for all people.

It's a fact, some twenty-six major denominations, including the Assemblies of God, Four Square, Church of God in Christ, Church of God –Cleveland Tennessee, Apostolic Faith, United Pentecostal Church, and Pentecostal Assemblies of the World, all trace their roots to the Azusa Street Revival; and 700 denominations, including independent denominations.

Ambassadors Gwyneth Williams and Star Williams are blessed to have Bishop Otis G. Clark as father and grandfather. Seldom when a chronicle is written are the readers privileged to have "first-hand" information. Bishop Clark knew many of the original "saints" and now recalls the events in the pages of this book.

Join with me as we recount the events of the Azusa Mission. They are excited to have this privilege to retrace the roots of this move as we endeavor to complete what God started in 1906. Let us through these pages find the true spirit of Azusa, the spirit of unity.

1

The Holiness Movement

Contributions of The Movement

The Church's main concern should not be about membership but salvation. The revivals that have taken place during the nineteenth and twentieth centuries were responsible for salvations as well as restorations.

During the last two hundred years there have been several renewals, reformations and revivals.[1] In the sixteenth century, the Lutheran church was strong in their persuasion. After the Lutheran Church took her stand, the Catholic Church in Europe began to lose some credence.[2] The Puritans experienced a revival under Oliver Cromwell, John Bunyan, John Newton, and the Wesleyan Church worked with them. The Wesleyan church helped England, while France was fighting the revolution.[3]

During the nineteenth century, people experienced wonderful experiences under Charles G. Finney and Dwight L. Moody. In 1860, 23% of the American population attended some sort of church assembly.[4] Within the Methodist church in the North and South; there was an interest to return to the holiness movement that was prevalent in the United States in 1858.[5]

The movement made major contributions that prepared the groundwork for the Pentecostal uprising. The first was experiences following the crisis-experience of salvation, and the second was that it produced another remarkable wave in history that included the baptism of the Holy Spirit."

In 1870, the bishops of the south called for a restoration of sanctification. The bishops strongly emphasized that nothing was needed more than sanctification during that period. The return to sanctification would focus on biblical truths and possibly bring forth a renewal.[6] They called the doctrine "the three works of grace," but many Christians ignored it because of their interest in the "social Gospel."

The holiness movement became solid and staunch in its beliefs.[7] The movement was very independent and not easily accepted by other denominations. This movement was traced back to its beginning in Vineland, New Jersey at a camp meeting on July 17, 1867.[8] The focus of the meeting was to "exert an influence over all of Christendom," about holiness and "to bring forth a new era in Methodism."[9]

Holiness Movement's Effects on Denominations

The movement also influenced other church denominations of the twentieth century. Vinson Synan, a scholar and writer, said, "Little did these men realize that this meeting would eventually result in the formation of over 14,000 denominations around the world and bring to birth a 'third force' in Christendom, the Pentecostal Movement."[10] Elmer T. Clark, author of The Small Sects in America, lists 60 separate Holiness and Pentecostal groups that came into existence between 1880 and 1930.[11]

The Holiness Church and Its Theology

The Holiness movement, in its theology, was consistent with the belief that there must be holiness, which comes from an inward channel, and that moral standards must be exemplified.[12] The intentions were not to directly create a new denomination, but to hold up biblical standards. The movement at the turn of the century began to reflect changes in the Church.

When the Azusa Street services took place, it was the beginning of a new wave of revival. The Pentecostal Movement rose out of the Holiness churches. The church stood for oneness of ethnic groups coming together in worship and love for each other. They stood against anti-semantic views against others and replacement theology.

The theological focuses were conversion, sanctification, unity and the God given ability to live a moral and clean life. Another focus was the baptism of the Holy Spirit, in which one was filled with God's Spirit and had value added to one's life. The Christians who wanted to be complete in their spiritual walk sought all three of these blessings.[13]

W.H. Durham's Theology

The theological commotion that led the Pentecostal movement to separate from the Holiness movement continued through the first two decades of the twentieth century. The "Jesus Only Controversy" was one source of conflict.[14] Another was the "finished work doctrine" of W.H. Durham,[15] who had also gone to Azusa Street and returned as a convert to the new Pentecostal doctrine. He was the pastor of a mission in Chicago, Illinois and was originally a Baptist preacher who later was a pastor of a small Holiness church near Houston, Texas. Durham called for a new view that assigned sanctification to the act of conversion based on the finished work of Christ on Calvary. Durham denied Wesley's view of sin dwelling in the believer.[16] He was the pastor of a mission in Chicago and was originally a Baptist although he preached the Wesleyan view of sanctification. In 1910, however, he arrived at a new theological position, calling his new doctrine, "The Finished Work."[17] Durham believed he was sanctified at conversion and did not need a second change later. It should be noted that this doctrine focuses on the position taken by the Southern Methodist church of 1894. The Methodist statement disputed the monopoly on truth claimed by the Holiness people. Durham's teaching, on the other hand, attacked the doctrinal basis of the Pentecostal movement and denied its claim to any truth.

In February of 1911, Durham arrived in Los Angeles, California; to present his new doctrine.[18] William J. Seymour founded the Azusa Mission in Los Angeles. In his absence, Durham taught at the Azusa mission. Large crowds attended, and controversy erupted because of the teachings. After Seymour returned, he requested that Durham reconsider teaching his new doctrine to the congregation. Durham declined, and as a result, a major split caused an unsettling at Azusa and within the Pentecostal movement.[19]

In July of 1912, at the age of thirty-nine, Durham died suddenly—some say he prophesied his own death. He stated, "If I ever leave the divine will, I will perish unexpectedly."[20] After Durham's death, in April 1913, his followers held a Worldwide Camp Meeting at the Azusa site. Nearly one thousand people attended the meeting, including Seymour, who attended as a spectator. Because of this meeting, the "oneness" or "Jesus Only" movement began.

2

The Pentecostal Revival

Charles Parham

Charles Parham was born in Muscatine, Iowa on June 4, 1873, and he became a Methodist minister as a young man.[21] Later he withdrew from the Methodists and associated himself with the Holiness circle. In October 1900, Parham opened a small Bible school in Topeka, Kansas, called Bethel Bible College.[22] Regarding this venture one writer stated, "Little did Parham realize that this school was to be the birthplace of the modern Pentecostal movement."

Parham started his school in 1898[23] and by 1901 had over forty people.[24] Many believe Parham was the first to teach on the glossolalia (tongues) movement.[25] He was considered the first leader of the revival and continued to hold a prominent place in it until his death in 1929.[26] Many people called him the "father of the Pentecostal Movement."

As the Azusa event started, Parham was considered the theological father of the event because of his teachings about the Holy Spirit. After returning from a trip, he noticed a change in the students. Parham stated, "To my astonishment, they all had the same story that while there were different things occurring when the Pentecostal blessing fell, the proof was that they spoke with other tongues.[27]

Parham returned home from the trip on December 31, 1900. He had each student study the Bible individually while he was away. They read and pondered the book of Acts. Parham questioned the students at a chapel service regarding the hypothesis they had reached.[28]

This event set in motion the greatest Pentecostal revivals in modern times, though these forty students did not realize this. The students had interpreted from the Scriptures that receiving tongues marked the reception of the Holy Spirit; tongues were the initial evidence of the indwelling of the Holy Spirit.[29] This realization made the Bible school students hungry to receive the same experience as the believers in Acts. This was the "first time," that speaking in tongues was considered the initial physical evidence of a person having received the baptism of the Holy Spirit.

Parham and the Pentecostal Movement

When Parham visited Azusa in 1906, he did not approve of what he found. He witnessed theological, interracial, and power struggles within the Azusa mission.[30] And when he attempted to redirect the people, he actually caused other church meetings to start.[31] However, despite the disagreements Parham noted, nothing would stop the move of the Holy Spirit. The modern Pentecostal Movement had been born. The Pentecostal Movement is a twentieth-century occurrence that emphasized growth and accompanied the increase of a new denomination—the Pentecostal church—particularly during the 1940's. (A new type of Pentecostalism promulgated since 1950.)[32]

Many people had a role to play in the Pentecostal outpouring, but Parham, Seymour, and Agnes Ozman—the first person known to speak in tongues—were the instruments that God used to cause the issue of a second work of grace, which was not received well. There was some turmoil over the issue between the Holiness and non-Holiness denominations. Some of these individuals later became Pentecostal.

Sanctification, the principle that defined the present Pentecostal view, was refined at Parham's school. Sanctification was not to be confused with the baptism of the Holy Spirit; it was a third experience separate in time and nature from the second blessing. Sanctification cleansed and purified the believer, while the baptism of the Holy Spirit" brought great power for service. The only Biblical evidence that one had received the baptism was the act of speaking with other tongues, as the 120 disciples had done on the day of Pentecost. The Pentecostals were not satisfied until they had spoken with tongues as proof that they had received the Holy Spirit.[33]

The Bible was the only textbook the forty students who enrolled at Bethel Bible College used. They studied the baptism of the Holy Spirit, for Parham was convinced that a great outpouring of power for Christians remained after sanctification. Parham gave the students an assignment—an exhaustive study of the Bible to explain the biblical evidence of the baptism in the Holy Spirit. After their studies, they were unanimous in their answer that "speaking in other tongues as the Spirit gives utterance was evidence of the Holy Spirit baptism."

Speaking in Glossolalia

Due to much prayer, fasting, and seeking, a young woman, Agnes N. Ozman, received an experience of speaking in glossolalia or tongues on January 1, 1901, at Bethel College.[34] Her fellow students prayed for her and laid hands on her head; she testified,

> The Holy Spirit fell upon me and I began to speak in tongues glorifying God. I talked in several languages. A few days later other students prayed, and one after another they began speaking in tongues and some were given the interpretation.

Some Church scholars consider this the birth of the modern Pentecostal movement.[35]

Parham's students had received from God's Word that during apostolic times speaking in tongues was considered the initial physical evidence that a person had received the baptism in the Holy Spirit. The whole group began the services on Watch Night, December 31, 1900, seeking the baptism of the Holy Spirit, with evidence by "ecstatic utterances in tongues." Ozman, gives the following account:

> On Watch Night, we had a blessed service, praying that God's blessings might rest upon us as the New Year came in. During the first day of 1901, the presence of the Lord was with us in a marked way, stilling our hearts to wait upon him for greater things. A spirit of prayer was upon us in the evening. It was nearly eleven o'clock. On this first of January that it came into my heart to ask that hands be laid upon me that I might receive the baptism of the Holy Spirit. As hands (Parham's) were laid upon my head the Holy Spirit came upon me, and I began to speak in tongues, glorifying God. I talked in several languages. It was as though rivers of living waters were going from my innermost being.[36]

The services continued over into the New Year. God's approval was there. The students prayed and sought His blessings. From this time (January 1, 1901), Pentecostal believers taught that the baptism in the Holy Spirit should be sought and that it came with the evidence of tongues. It was this decision that made the Pentecostal Movement of the twentieth century a great asset to the well-being of the Church.[37]

Twentieth Century Accounts of Glossolalia

Concerning Ozman's experiences, J. Roswell Flower, a Pentecostal leader, believes there could have been other events of people speaking in glossolalia.[38] According to Flower, there has been many instances of persons speaking in tongues before the year 1900, but in each case, the speaking in glossolalia was looked at as a strange spiritual occurrence or a gift of the Holy Spirit. There was no special emphasis given that would cause those seeking the fullness of the Spirit to expect that they should speak in other tongues.[39]

Stanley H. Frodsham, author of With Signs Following, believes that before the turn of the century people had "spoken with other tongues." He states, "Records suggest that people received the Holy Spirit and speaking in tongues before Pentecost in Los Angeles.

3

William J. Seymour

Seymour's Life

Pictured: William J. Seymour [175]

William Joseph Seymour was born in 1870, in Centerville, Louisiana.[40] Some of his close friends believed he was born during slavery.[41] Seymour's parents' names are unknown because he was separated from them early in his childhood. The last name Seymour was correct. This name was given in slavery as early as 1800-1860.[42] Seymour did not have much education. He loved the great "Negro spirituals," had visions of God, and became an apostle of God.

In 1895, Seymour went to Indianapolis, Indiana. There he joined the Methodist Episcopal church. This church had an outreach to blacks, but during this time Seymour tried to cause interracial reconciliation.

In 1900, Seymour moved to Cincinnati, Ohio. There he became a part of the Church of God Reformation Movement (Evening Light Saints), and this church was the most progressive interracial church in America at the time. During this time, he became ill with smallpox. He thought this was because he disobeyed the call to ministry. Some report that facial scars and the loss of sight in one eye resulted from his illness, though other accounts say that he was not blind in his one eye. During this time, he received ministerial credentials from the Evening Light Saints and became an evangelist. In 1903, he moved to Houston to look for relatives that had been separated during slavery days. Shortly afterwards, Seymour resumed spreading the Gospel and evangelizing.[43]

Seymour and Parham

In 1905, Parham held meetings in downtown Houston, Texas. Black holiness pastor Lucy Farrow was Parham's governess. She went on a trip with Parham and asked Seymour to preach at her church. When she returned from the trip, she told Seymour about glossolalia.[44]

Seymour and Parham, between 1901 and 1905, spread the Pentecostal doctrine through Kansas, Missouri, Oklahoma, and Texas. Because of successful revivals held in and around Houston, Parham opened a Bible school there in December 1905. Seymour was the only black holiness preacher who attended the newly established Bible school in Houston, Texas. Seymour and Parham preached together in the black section of downtown Houston in the afternoons. During the evenings, Seymour and the other blacks had to sit in the back of the meetings they had downtown. Due to the segregation policies, they were not allowed to help at the altar or sit in the front.

Seymour went to Los Angeles, California in the spring of 1906.[45] He became one of history's most prominent leaders in the Azusa revival. The revival in Los Angeles strongest services lasted for three and half years but continued until 1919. There was always some kind of meeting taking place. They were held in a Methodist church that was later known as the Azusa Mission. From California, the Pentecostal revival spread throughout the world. "Out of this widespread interest in Pentecostalism, several groups emerged as fully organized religious bodies."[46]

Donald Metz, a modern writer, describes the Pentecostal movement as a significant event and likens it to "another Pentecost." He believes the Christian body will recognize the manifestation that took place in this century.[47] Some would reply that there are some reasons for reluctance and don't identify with the Azusa movement.

It was God's ordained will for Seymour to enroll in Parham's school. They ministered together during the day sessions, even though the evening sessions when they ministered downtown, Parham would not let the blacks minister because of the segregation policies. God still worked things out for His good.[48] Despite the conflicts and confrontations, many lives were transformed.

Seymour and Julia Hutchinson

In 1906, Seymour was invited to preach in a Nazarene church in Los Angeles where Julia Hutchison was the pastor.[49] When Seymour preached his first sermon proclaiming the "initial evidence" theory of the baptism in the Holy Spirit he was locked out of the church.

In 1906, Hutchinson, a member of a black Baptist church, began teaching holiness and sanctification as separate works of grace, besides a born-again experience. Other members also believed this doctrine. The pastor expelled eight families from the church.

Hutchison's followers, which included Ruth and Richard Asberry, opened a mission on Santa Fe Street in Los Angeles. There they could worship God as they felt the Spirit leading them.

Hutchinson felt the congregation should have a man as assistant pastor. Neely Terry went to Houston, Texas and had just returned from her visit. There she had met Seymour who came to the mission.[50] His fare was paid and sent to him, so he could travel to Los Angeles. His first sermon was on the baptism of the Holy Spirit, a subject he had heard preached on in a tent meeting in Houston. The tiny congregation accepted both the man and his message, but Hutchinson immediately put a padlock on the Nazarene mission because she was not receptive to Seymour's doctrine.

Pictured: William J. Seymour[176]

Seymour and Edward S. Lee

After Seymour left the Nazarene meeting, Edward Lee, a member of the Peniel Mission, invited Seymour to his home for dinner. Lee, out of respect, took Seymour into his home. Although he did not believe in his doctrine, he did not want to leave Seymour on the street without any money.

After being in Lee's home a few nights, Seymour asked for them to pray with him. Shortly afterwards, Lee and his wife felt better about Seymour.[51] God dealt with the hearts of the other saints as well, and they began to come around and pray with Seymour, even though they did not agree with his teaching. Ruth Asberry came to the meetings. The Asberry's asked Seymour to hold the meeting in their home.[52]

At this time, Lee was in constant prayer.[53] Two men appeared to him one day while he was praying on his job in the basement of a bank. The two men were Peter and John. They stood and looked at him, then their hands arose to heaven, and they began to quiver under the power of God and began to speak in tongues.[54]

Lee said, "I jumped up, and I was just shaking under the power of God, and I did not know what was the matter." That evening, Seymour explained to the group of people that were listening to Lee's testimony that this was a manifestation of the Holy Spirit.

After hearing Lee's testimony of the vision, the people had an innate desire to receive an experience with the Holy Spirit. Shortly afterwards, Lee asked Seymour to lay hands upon him, so he could receive the baptism of the Holy Spirit. Seymour said, "The Lord wants me to lay hands suddenly on no man." But, later that evening, Seymour prayed for Lee, and he went out under the power of God. Lee's wife was frightened and did not understand what happened. Lee got up after a few minutes; he had received a heavenly touch.[55]

Seymour met Lucy Farrow in Texas. She taught about Acts 2:4. After Seymour told the group about her, they gathered the money and sent for her. One evening after Farrow had arrived, she laid hands on Lee, and he fell out of his chair as the Spirit fell.[56] It seemed that he had fainted. When he got up, he spoke in other tongues.[57]

Pictured: Bonnie Brae House, the home where the Azusa Revival began[177]

Bonnie Brae Street

The little band of black truth seekers who had been expelled from one building and locked out of another were still meeting at Ruth and Richard Asberry.

After Lee received the baptism in the Holy Spirit that evening, they went to the prayer meeting on Bonnie Brae Street. When Lee walked into the house, other people were there praying on their knees. The power of God hit Lee and he began to speak in tongues.

This occurred on April 9, 1906. The others were seated in the living room in a spirit of prayer and were waiting upon the Lord. Suddenly, as if hit by a bolt of lightning from heaven, they were all knocked from their chairs to the floor; many began speaking with other tongues. Among these were Jennie Moore, Brother Hughes, Sister Traynor and her son, Bud, and Sister Crawford's daughter. Willella Asberry rushed from the kitchen to see what was happening in the living room. Young Bud Traynor was on the front porch, prophesying and preaching. Moore stood up and prophesied in what the others called Hebrew. Then she went to the piano and for the first time in her life, she began playing beautiful music, singing in a beautiful language and voice. She never lost these gifts, and the piano was in the cottage at 216 Bonnie Brae Street for years but was moved to Pisgah. Currently, the original table and Kathryn Kuhlman's pulpit are at the mission. Clark stated upon a visit in 2010 how he had been in the house and eaten at the table on several occasions.

The next morning people came from everywhere. There was no way of getting near the house. Those that got in fell under the power of the Holy Spirit as they entered or came near the house. The people shouted for three days and nights and stirred the whole city of Los Angeles. During these three days people were saved and many received the baptism of the Holy Spirit.[58] Ruth Asberry and Jennie Moore went to Peniel Hall in Los Angeles—the same location it is today. Moore spoke in tongues and Ruth explained: "This is that which was prophesied by Joel." The crowd followed them to Azusa Street, and the great rush was on. Shortly afterwards, a great revival broke forth.[59]

California Meetings

The home prayer meetings soon gave way and the front porch became the pulpit. The street became the pews that drew hundreds of eager listeners who came to hear Seymour and his tongue-speaking followers. Soon the crowds became so numerous that larger facilities were needed for the fast-growing group.

They conducted a vast search of the downtown Los Angeles area and found an abandoned old building at 312 Azusa Street. The building had been used previously as a Methodist church, a stable, and a warehouse. It was in shambles. The windows and doors were out, and debris littered the place. The band of Pentecostals who began holding services there in April of 1906 felt as though the facility was appropriate. Converts, both whites and blacks, overflowed the building. The old deserted two-story building was at a dead-end street only about a half block long in the industrial section of downtown Los Angeles.

Seymour resided in California for the remainder of his life. His teaching was new and offensive to some. Mostly, all Christians claimed to be filled with the Holy Spirit without the initial evidence of speaking in tongues. The teaching of glossolalia became the centerpiece of Pentecostal teaching with Seymour as the "apostle" of the movement. Tent meetings, missions, and churches were so empty that some closed and joined the movement.

Pictured: The Azusa Street Mission Building where many people flocked to experience the power of the Holy Spirit.[178]

Renovation of Azusa

The upstairs of the Azusa Mission was the tarrying room, but many received their baptism just sitting in the lower services. Hundreds of eager and excited people were there to receive what Seymour was teaching. On April 9, 1906, a Pentecostal revival began with the manifestations that characterized those in the Midwest. Swiftly the Los Angeles phenomena spread across the country.

Arthur G. Osterberg, a minister that worked for J.V. McNeil Company in Los Angeles was an attender of a Full Gospel Church.[60] Osterberg was impressed with Seymour and helped him renovate the Azusa Mission. He was a foreman and he used his men to help prepare the old building for service. The J.V. McNeil Company is presently the McNeil Construction Company and is one of the largest on the Pacific coast. Two people helped Seymour financially get the building appropriate for the church meetings.[61]

People had discarded quite a volume of trash at the mission. They put down sawdust on the floor, bought kegs of nails, and made wooden benches. They stacked two wooden shoeboxes on top of one another and used for a pulpit. J.V. McNeill, a devout Catholic, also gave wood for an altar.[62]

The services then moved from Bonnie Brae Street to Azusa Street. The meetings were fiery, but there was freedom to praise God. Visiting ministers were given the freedom to express God. People prayed and shouted while others fell out under the power of the Holy Spirit; there were extended moments of silence and singing in tongues.

The upstairs areas of the Azusa Mission doubled as an office for several residents, including Seymour and later his wife. It was difficult to handle the overflow at the altar, and they used the upstairs for that. High on the agenda of most of those who tarried was a Pentecostal baptism in the Spirit and the ability to speak in tongues.

Seymour Makes Request for Credentials

Seymour believed greatly in what was happening at the mission. He knew that it was something important and new, but he sought first to acknowledge its relationship with the work of Parham. In July 1906 he wrote to W. F. Carruthers, field secretary, asking for promised ministerial credentials from Parham. Carruthers sent the note on to Parham, remarking the he had filled the request.

Seymour Speaks in Glossolalia

Strange as it may seem, some report that Seymour did not speak in tongues until sometimes after Azusa began. However, Seymour and his mission gained increasing respect and notoriety. The Azusa Mission spread in part through first hand testimonies and through The Apostolic Faith newspaper that was published between September 1906 and May 1908 by members of the Azusa mission staff.

Seymour's Preaching Style and Order of Service

Seymour generally sat behind the two empty shoeboxes that were used for shipping. He usually kept his head inside the top one during the meeting while praying. Seymour was a humble man and did not want to reveal any pride. The services ran almost any hour, night and day. The Azusa Mission was never closed or empty. The people came to meet God. He was always there. Therefore, a continuous meeting progressed as the people bathed in His presence. The meetings did not always depend on a human leader. God's presence became more wonderful in that old building, with its low rafters and bare floors. God met the people there.

Seymour had become a sort of moderator. He was a marvelous teacher of the deep things of God, and usually he sat with his head bowed inside the shoebox pulpit while God carried on the meeting. Those anointed to preach were always welcome and allowed to participate. As many as nine services were held in one day. The meetings continued day and night, around the clock. People would come in and kneel and pray, then sit with their eyes closed and quietly wait for God to work. Two favorite songs were, "Under the Blood" and "The Comforter is Come." Singing in the Spirit was glorious. It sounded like a perfect heavenly choir. The newcomers were awed by the flow of the Spirit. Prophecies, messages, and interpretations were given with convicting power, as though the Lord Himself was speaking directly. Conversions, the baptism of the Holy Spirit, miraculous healings, seeking lost souls and casting out demons became regular procedures. The power could be felt even five blocks away.

No subjects or sermons were ever announced and there were no special speakers. No one knew what might happen or what God would do. All was spontaneous, ordered of the Spirit.[63] They wanted to hear from God, through whomever He might be using, and experience what God would do. The rich and educated were the same as the poor and uninformed. All were equal; they only recognized God. No flesh could get glory in His presence. He could not use the self-opinionated. Those were Holy Ghost meetings, led of the Lord. It had to start in poor surroundings, to keep out the selfish, human elements. All came down in humility together, at His feet. They all looked alike and had all things in common in that sense at least. By the time they got to Azusa they were humbled, ready for the blessing. The Spirit, from the throne of God, controlled the meetings. Those were truly wonderful days. Seymour often said, "I would rather live six months serving God to the fullness than fifty years of ordinary life."

Pictured: William J. Seymour and wife Jennie Moore.[179]

Seymour Marries & Conflict Arises

Seymour later married Jennie Evan Moore.[64] She was an original Azusa member. Jennie did some traveling with Seymour after the marriage, but she was also an evangelist before she married Seymour. She was known for her powerful and unique speaking. She had a beautiful singing voice and was known as a great cook. She worked hard and missed some of the Sunday services, so she could work to help provide for the churches expenses. Normally, she would write a letter of encouragement to the congregation they would read at the services she missed.

Clara Lum, the main administrator for the newspaper "Apostolic Faith," did not believe there was time for marrying and giving in marriage. Because Seymour made the decision to get married, she disregarded the trustee's warnings and departed, taking the important national and international mailing lists. The only mailing list that was left was the local Los Angeles one.

Seymour refused to take any type of legal action to regain the lists. He tried to continue to publish the paper without the list but was unsuccessful. Without the effect of the newspaper, Seymour and Azusa Street slowly declined.

Pictured: Revivalist, William J. Seymour

Seymour the Central Figure

The official beginning of the Pentecostal movement is usually traced to one of two sources. The Azusa Street revival in Los Angeles in 1906, in which Seymour was the central figure, or the Bible school operated by Charles Parham in Topeka, Kansas, from 1900 to 1901. Bishop Otis G. Clark continued the legacy, after Seymour's homegoing in 1922, until he was 109.

Parham's school and teaching achieved widespread popularity, but the famous Azusa Street Revival caused his teaching to sweep the world. The practices reported at the revival he opened did not seem to be different from those of the conventional Holiness revival. Although speaking in tongues was explicitly associated with the baptism of the Spirit as a doctrinal principle. The people shouted, wept, danced, fell into trances, spoke and sang in tongues and interpreted the messages in English.[65] The revival continued at Azusa Street for three years and six months. During this time the meetings were 24 hours a day and seven days a week. The revival was consistent until 1919. In the first years news of it rapidly spread throughout the city and around the country. In the south many became familiar with the revival through the regular reports of Frank Bartleman in the "Way of Faith" newspaper. The "Apostolic Faith" papers circulated by Seymour went to over 50,000 homes.

God used Seymour who was to become the leader of the movement in Los Angeles. He was a good pastor and was committed to his call until his death in 1922. Seymour believed in desegregation and had many white and black followers. It was reported that in the beginning of Azusa, blacks were the majority. When the ministry grew it was reported to have more whites. Later, the whites began to start their own organizations in Los Angeles and records indicated that blacks were predominate at the mission.[66]

Pictured: Bishop Otis Clark, with daughter and grand-daughter, Ambassadors Dr. Gwyneth & Star at Seymour's grave site and at 312 Azusa Street

4

Testimonies of Azusa

NAMES OF INDIVIDUALS FROM LEFT TO RIGHT. UPPER ROW STANDING (1), (UNKNOWN), (2) BROTHER EVANS, THE FIRST MAN TO RECEIVE THE BAPTISM; JENNIE MOORE; WHO AFTERWARDS MARRIED BROTHER SEYMOUR; GLENN A. COOK, SISTER CRAWFORD, WHO BUILT UP A LARGE WORK IN PORTLAND, OREGON, (UNKNOWN), SISTER PRINCE, KNOWN AS A MOTHER IN ISRAEL. LOWER ROW SEATED, SISTER EVANS, THE FIRST WOMAN TO RECEIVE THE BAPTISM, BROTHER HIRAM SMITH, A GREAT HELP IN THE BUSINESS OF THE MISSION, WILLIAM JOSEPH SEYMOUR, THE CHEIF APOSTLE AND FOUNDER OF THE AZUSA MOVEMENT, CLARA LUM, STENOGRAPHER, AND WONDERFUL HELPER IN EDITING THE PAPER, AND SPREADING THE GOOD NEWS ALL OVER THE WORLD. SISTER CRAWFORD'S CHILD.

Pictured: William J. Seymour and key Azusa Mission leaders.[180]

William Seymour, Azusa Pentecostals and her sister the Charismatic movements main emphasis was the New Testament church. The book of Acts was prevalent. The fruits and gifts of the Spirit were manifest. The Azusa outpouring was known for its testimonials or witness of the signs wonders and miracles. Thousands of people were inspired, encouraged, and faith increased by the testimonies. Daily in the services people would share what the Holy Spirit did in their lives. Many times, they would start off the testimony by saying,"' I believe I will testify while I have a chance, or we overcome by the Blood of the lamb and the Word of our testimony. Many people were healed of cancer, sicknesses and diseases.

People gave testimony of God's goodness and the Baptism of the Holy Spirit. Acts 1:8 Jesus telling the disciples that they are to be His "witnesses" this means giving testimony to what they have experienced through the power of Christ.

Williams states, when she was a child, they would always have testimony service. When she was a teenager she would lead the testimony service at the church. What would happen, anyone who had a "testimony" could stand up and tell their story.

When the saints, as we called them then would stand up and tell about the goodness and how Jesus in their daily life did something extraordinary, signs, wonders, deliverance, and miracles. The book of Acts was alive in the services. The fire of God, open heavens and the shekinah glory.

People would shout and scream "Hallelujah!" Their hearts were filled with the Holy Spirit, joy and the fire of God. Their testimonies took the fire of the Holy Spirit to the nations of the world

Matthew 28:16-20: "So the eleven disciples went to Galilee to the mountain Jesus had designated. When they saw Him, they worshiped Him. Then Jesus came up and said to them, "All authority in heaven and on earth has been given to me. Therefore, go and make disciples of all nations, baptizing them in the name of the

Father and the Son and the Holy Spirit, teaching them to obey everything I have commanded you. And remember, I am with you always, to the end of the age."

J. Roswell Flower

The review of the prominent Pentecostal leader, J. Roswell Flower said, "I shall never forget the day when the first messengers from Azusa Street in Los Angeles came into the community in which I lived."[67] Flower shared his Pentecostal experience. His experiences were scriptural and based on Acts 2:4. He spoke in tongues and was baptized with the Holy Spirit. He proclaimed the goodness of God fervently and with excitement. He was thirsty for living water and a fresh rhema word and experience from God.

Christians wanted something more than teaching. They wanted an experience with the true and living God. God met the people where their faith was. This event took place in Indianapolis, Indiana and hundreds of others received a similar blessing.[68]

T.B. Barrett

T.B. Barrett (1862-1940), a Norwegian Methodist pastor, heard about the Pentecostal outpouring that was taking place in Los Angeles, while he was in New York City. Barrett wrote the Azusa Mission in Los Angeles. He received their counsel and obtained a clear view of the baptism in the Holy Spirit. He later went to England, Norway, Germany, and Sweden to set up Pentecostal churches.[69] He was known as the European father of the Pentecostal Movement.

People came from all over the world to Los Angeles. Within less than a generation, Pentecostalism was "a force to be reckoned with throughout the world."[70]

Also, using testimonies from early Pentecostal leaders, Barret expounded upon a book by a man who had contact with the emerging Pentecostalism from 1909 onwards. He did not embrace Barret's own position. He stated, "Speaking with tongues is certainly Pentecostal, nor do I question that the Spirit of God can grant this power today."[71] Barret did not approve of the thought that gifts were not for this time. He believed in the miraculous and the manifestation of the gifts. Barrett was not biased at all about the subject of Pentecost.[72]

There are some prophetic words that did not meet Barrett's approval. He drew upon his own experiences and obtained information from articles and magazines written about Azusa. Barrett paints a picture that is very disturbing to some who have not experienced the supernatural; especially since most of the evidence is from Pentecostals.[73]

Before Barrett received his baptism, he consecrated himself before God and sought the gift. It was recorded that shortly afterwards he had a special manifestation in his jaws and tongue.[74] When it happened, he declared that someone saw a crown of fire over his head and a cloven tongue as of fire in front of the crown, and soon he was lying on the floor with his eyes shut, speaking in many languages. He claimed there were approximately seven or eight different languages, until there was an ache in his vocal chords.[75]

The highly charged atmosphere and the undoubtedly remarkable events did not obscure the simple fact that all kinds of strange occurrences happened. These events were totally different from Pentecost, simply because it was in no way a repetition of the Pentecostal event. Another experience, there were only fifteen people in a room, Barrett was led to bellow forth words at top volume: "I know from the strength of my voice that 10,000 might easily have heard all I said."[76]

Moreover, about his claim that he was divinely inspired, words would rush forth like a waterfall, and it seemed as if an iron hand was laid over his jaws.

It was reported that both his jaws and tongue sounded different from his normal voice. This was the manifestation of the Spirit's work. Barrett was an example of a balance of the early days of the movement.[77] According to Victor Budgen, The Charismatics and the Word of God his reports were people were walking about the hall and playing the piano with their eyes closed.[78] Other incidents included public weeping, shouting, dancing, leaping, and laying in a heap on the podium before the congregation. There were people falling backwards across the steps and were slain by the power of God, but some were astonished just like the day of Pentecost. People thought they were drunk in the book of Acts, and some people did not understand God's power and the incidents happening then.

Emma Cotton Mother of Azusa

Emma Cotton born 1877 and departed this earth December 27, 1952, she was a famous evangelist and preacher born of Creole of descent in the United States, in Louisiana. Cotton portrayed the Azusa meetings as somewhat odd and different. Cotton received the baptism of the Holy Spirit at the Azusa Mission and told Clark and others about the events upon his arrival in 1921 and her return to Los Angeles in 1920.

Clark was introduced to Cotton by my grandfather Henry Clark. He was a deacon at the First Baptist Church on Bonnie Brae. The church was located during that time across from the Bonnie Brae home where the prayer meetings were held prior to moving to the building on Azusa Street. Otis Clark lived in her home, was her driver and collaborator in the ministry. Clark would go with her to evangelistic healing services, help oversee churches in San Jose, Oakland, Fresno, Bakersfield and other churches in the United States. They planted churches, visited many of the churches opened during the Azusa Revival and after Seymour's death. Clark became the Timothy to Mother Cotton

She was the founder of the Azusa Temple as well as other Pentecostal churches across the United States. Cotton's preaching and involvement in the Pentecostal circuit, as well as her friendship with famous evangelist, Aimee Semple McPherson, paved the way for women in church leadership in the 1900's. McPherson died in September 1944. Clark told us of many meetings with Cotton and McPherson. He loved to tell the story of how she would kiss him on the cheek and give him a white rose. Also, giving out roses was one of the things she would do during baptism.

In addition, he was in business meetings where McPherson would give Cotton money to keep Azusa open. The original Azusa Street building was demolished in 1931. Seymour's wife, Jennie E. Seymour tried to keep the church open, but later died in 1936. Many independent Pentecostal denominations were beginning to develop.

Cotton and Clark continued to share about the Azusa outpouring. She believed tongues were associated with the baptism of the Spirit as a doctrinal principle. She sang, preached, and rejoiced freely in the Spirit and was a respected black pastor who established several churches. She was a legend and appeared in history in 1906 during the Azusa Street Revival and worked until her death in 1952.

Many people were saved and baptized with the Holy Spirit under her ministry. She relayed that Seymour seemed the nominal leader, humble and he usually kept his head inside the top of his two shoeboxes that were used as his pulpit during the meetings, praying. Cotton said, "Sometimes the enemy would come in and bind the services. There were some women that prayed and interceded for the meetings until the services were freed." Cotton told testimonies of the events to Otis G. Clark and others before he arrived in 1921. She said, "The meetings reported at the revival Seymour opened in Los Angeles were different." Mother Emma and Henry Cotton were instrumental in having the 30th year Azusa Street Revival anniversary. Clark helped with the event. The meeting was held at Aimee Semple McPhersons church in Los Angeles, California.

Did Azusa Fail?

Azusa began to reflect some lukewarm ways when the ministry began to stress structure.[79] Budgen also stated, "When the movement developed, stages were built higher, coat tails were worn longer, choirs were organized, and string bands came into existence to jazz the people. The kings came back again." The church began to separate; exegetical and hermeneutical discussions were prevalent.

Seymour was humble, and while he kept his head inside the old empty box at Azusa, all was well. "Now we know what the remedy is for preserving spiritual Eden. Keeping the preacher with his head in a shoebox."[80] They knew God must be the center of attention and the main focus. It is humility that will help the Church to rise like an island in the sea. "Next in importance to the doctrine of the preacher with his head in a box comes the doctrine of lying on the floor!"[81]

Azusa Spreading Abroad: Ministers and Workers From Distant Lands

Cotton also told about an Englishman who came from London, England, though she never learned his name. He came across the ocean to attend the Azusa meetings. God baptized him with the Holy Spirit, and he gave a great sum of money to pay off the church's debts. He then returned to England with his wonderful experience of the baptism of the Holy Spirit. This outpouring spread to many parts of the world.

The work was getting clearer and stronger at Azusa. God was working mightily, and it seemed that everyone that went to Los Angeles had to go to Azusa. Missionaries gathered there from Africa, India, and the islands of the sea. Preachers and workers crossed the continents, and some came from distant islands.[82] It was as though God was saying, "Gather my saints together" (Ps.50:1-7). They had come up for Pentecost, though they may not have realized it. It was God's call and will for them to be there.

Holiness meetings, tents, and missions began to close for lack of attendance because the people were at Azusa. The Garr's closed the Burning Bush Hall to attend. There they received the baptism and were soon on their way to India to spread the fire. Pastor Smale had to come to Azusa to look up his members. He invited them back home and promised them liberty in the Spirit, and for a time God moved mightily in the New Testament Church, also.

A missionary from Los Angeles went to Liberia, Africa and spoke to the people in the Cru language. Another person wrote in an unknown language under the power of the Spirit, and it was understood and read by the kings in Africa.[83]

Believers from all over the world benefited from what God did at Azusa. The people at the Azusa Mission happily received the messages that people in Calcutta, India had received the baptism of the Holy Spirit. People also wrote from China, Germany, Switzerland, Norway, Sweden, England, Ireland, Australia, and other countries. Some of these letters were in foreign languages. Missionaries wrote that they were hungry for this outpouring of the Spirit, which they believed to be the real Pentecost.[84] The world was ripe for the Pentecost that God sent. People all over the world were receptive to God's plan.

The Purchase of The Azusa Mission

The Apostolic Faith Mission purchased the lot and building at 312 Azusa Street. Five holy men were elected as trustees for the property. They believed the Lord chose that spot for His work, for He wonderfully poured out His Spirit on the mission.[85]

They purchased the property for $15,000. By 1907, $4,000 had already been paid on it. The mission was centrally located and in surroundings where no one would be disturbed by praying or shouting—which sometimes went on all night. During 1906, the Apostolic Faith paper reported that hundreds were saved, sanctified, healed, and baptized with the Holy Ghost.[86]

Pentecost in San Francisco

In San Francisco, God touched Hawaiians and Filipinos. There were striking cases both of conversion and sanctification and some remarkably clear cases of the divine baptism.[87] Five people were converted one night and a Hawaiian man and a Filipinos were gloriously converted. The Filipino said, "Me no speak English much, but me know God. Jesus, He got my heart." The Hawaiian could not speak for some time after he rose to his feet, because the power of God was so strongly upon him.

Andrew H. Argues' Letter to Azusa

A.H. Argue was a prominent person in the development of the Pentecostal Assemblies of Canada. In addition, he published the Apostolic Messenger which was a periodical for the Pentecostal Church published in 1908. Argue wrote to the Azusa Mission from Canada, he was founder and pastor of Calvary Temple in Winnipeg. He gave testimony of how he had returned from what he called a Pentecostal trip. The first place Argue visited was Toronto, Canada, where he enjoyed the fellowship of the saints.

Pentecost had fallen in at least five missions in San Francisco. From there, reports spread about Ottawa, Canada, and Athens, Greece where meetings were held, and there were some remarkable cases of conversion, sanctification, and the Pentecostal baptism. God truly was with Argue, and everyone rejoiced in the marvelous way in which God poured out His Spirit on his trips.

After sixteen days in Athens, the Lord permitted Argue to return home by way of New York City.[88] While Argue was there, twenty-five received the baptism in one week and five of the saints fasted for ten days. Pentecost fell on other missions in New York and nearby cities in Philadelphia, Baltimore, and Washington, D.C.[89] God saved many people on Argue's trip.[90]

Watson Argue continued the legacy of his father. He became the pastor of the church in Winnipeg, Canada. His leadership expanded the borders of the mission outreach. He knew about training nationals and this outreach truly left a legacy. Upon Dr. Gwyneth and Ambassador Star Williams visit to Uganda and East Africa. Many of the churches were influenced by Pentecostal Assemblies of Canada. They were so inspired by the Azusa legacy that is continuing.

Pictured: Charles Harrison Mason, Church of God in Christ Founder, received the Baptism in the Holy Spirit at the Azusa Mission.[181]

Charles H. Mason Receives Baptism at Azusa

Charles Mason received the baptism of the Holy Spirit at Azusa. He later became the founder of the Church of God in Christ. Charles Harrison Mason was born September 8, 1866, on the Prior farm near Memphis, Tennessee. His father's name was Jerry Mason and his mother's name was Eliza Mason.[91] They were members of a Missionary Baptist Church.

The people heard about Azusa in the south and in Mississippi. Mason came along with others C.P. Jones, J.A. Jeter, D. J. Young, and some of them were among the first members of Azusa Street Mission.

The first day Mason attended Azusa, he saw and heard something that did not look scriptural to him. He had begun to thank God in his heart for all things when he heard some speak in tongues. He knew it was right, though he did not understand it.

Mason gave a testimony, thanking Seymour, who came and preached a wonderful sermon. Seymour's words were gentle but powerful. At the meeting Seymour said, "All of those that want to be sanctified or baptized with the Holy Ghost, go to the upper room. All those that want to be healed, go to the prayer room. And those that want to be justified, come to the altar." Mason said, "That is the place for me, for it may be that I am not converted, and, if not, God knows it and can convert me."[92]

Satan spoke to Mason and said, If you get converted, will you tell me? Mason replied, "Yes," for he knew if he were not convinced and God did convert him, it would tell for itself. "I stood on my feet while waiting at the altar fearing someone would bother me, but I said in my mind, that if I ever get to that altar and get my back turned on the people, I will receive what God has for me."[93]

When Mason bowed down at the altar, someone called him and said, "Seymour wants you three brethren in his office." J.A. Jeter of Little Rock, Arkansas, and D. J. Young of Pine Bluff, Arkansas accompanied Mason. The three of them went up, and Seymour received them and was happy they were there. Seymour said, "Brethren, the Lord will do great things for us and bless us." He cautioned them not to run around in the city seeking worldly pleasure but to seek the will and pleasures of the Lord.

That night, God spoke to Mason that Jesus saw all the wrong things in the world but did not attempt to set it right until God overshadowed Him with the Holy

Spirit. Mason recounted God's words, "I was no better than my Lord, and if I wanted Him to baptize me, I would have to let the people's rights and wrongs alone and look to Him and not to the people, and He would baptize me.

Mason said yes to God, for it was God who wanted to baptize him and not the people. God spoke to him the next night.

The second night at Azusa, Mason saw a vision of himself standing alone with a dry roll of paper. He was chewing the paper. When all the paper was in his mouth, he tried to swallow it. When Mason looked up to Heaven, there was a man at his side. Then he turned his eyes and woke up.

The interpretation came to him. He stated, "God had me swallowing the whole book, and that if I did not turn my eyes to anyone but God and Him only, He would baptize me. I said yes to Him, and at once in the morning when I arose I could hear a voice saying, 'I see.'"[94] Mason later became the Chief Apostle and founder of the Church of God in Christ.

5

Newspaper Reports

Apostolic Faith Newspaper

In September 1906, Seymour published a letter in the Azusa Mission's newspaper The Apostolic Faith. In a particular article, Charles Parham told of his plans to visit the mission. The letter from Parham arrived from Tonganoxie, Kansas. He informed the mission that he would arrive on September 15th.[95] He informed them that he heard about the Pentecostal outpouring in Los Angeles. He stated,

> I rejoice in God over you all, my children, though I have never seen you: but since you know the Holy Spirit's power, we are baptized into one body. Keep together in unity till I come, then in a grand meeting let all prepare for the outside fields. I want unless God directs to the contrary to meet and see all who have the full Gospel when I come.[96]

The following month, Seymour acknowledged that the message of Pentecost had been preached ever since Agnes Ozman's experiences in Parham's Topeka, Kansas Bible school in 1901. Now, however, it had burst out in great power and was being carried worldwide from the Pacific Coast.

L.A. Times Reports

The meetings first began on Bonnie Brae Street and then followed to the premises on Azusa Street. The Los Angeles Times first reported the Azusa story in April of 1906. Calling tongues, a "weird babble" and Seymour's followers, "a sect of fanatics," the front-page of the Times' article created curiosity and bigger crowds for the meetings.[97] The "press wrote us up shamefully," declared Bartleman, "but that only drew more crowds."[98] The following is part of the Times report:

> Breathing strange utterances and mouthing a creed that it seems no sane mortal could understand, the newest religious sect has started in Los Angeles. Meetings are held in a tumbledown shack on Azusa Street, near San Pedro Street, and devotees of the weird doctrine practice the most fanatical rite, preach the wildest theories and work themselves into a state of mind excitement in their peculiar zeal. Black people and a sprinkle of whites compose the congregation, and night is made hideous in the neighborhood by the howling of the worshipers who spend hours swaying forth and back in a nerve racking attitude of prayer and supplication. They claim to have "gift of tongues," and to be able to comprehend the babel.[99]

Reports of Seymour and Parham

Parham arrived in Los Angeles on September 15, 1906. Parham came to Azusa to greet the people and preach the Word, and Seymour and his followers considered him a father in the Gospel. Seymour and Parham's relationship broke during October, 1906.[100]

Parham's sermons were not very easy for the Azusa fellowship to accept. He felt as though things were not being carried out correctly at the mission.[101] Because of his attempt to correct things, he was asked to leave the church. This event caused and interference in Parham and Seymour's relationship. According to Vinson Synan, the relationship was never healed.[102]

The revival continued for another three and one-half years at Azusa, with three services a day—morning, afternoon, and night. Most people came to receive the gift of tongues, but many others came for healing. Often times, interpretation followed speeches in tongues. As time passed, Seymour and his followers claimed that God had restored all the gifts of the Spirit to the Church.[103]

The Wave Swept the World

During the revival there were spontaneous waves of God's glory.[104] The Azusa tide swept through the country and the world. Pentecost knocked on the doors of churches everywhere. The spirit of revival came upon the United States of America, and God and the Holy Spirit directed it.

The revival, however, was something that was not immediately apparent. Years later critics still proclaimed that what happened at Azusa was for only a short time, but actually it went until 1919. The three and a half years was 24 hours a day meetings. An observer, Carrie Judd Montgomery, whose husband George had visited Azusa in December of 1906, had come away with glowing reports of what God was doing there. It was reported that, "there was no real revival as a whole in Los Angeles, but only here and there some people were trusting God fully and receiving a rich experience of His grace." Even today the fruit of the revival has blessed every continent of the world.

For the most part, the reports were accurate depending on what days and time people attended. Yet the opening of the Azusa Street Mission was something that did not escape the eyes of many, including members of the secular press. The Los

Angeles Times sent a reporter to an evening meeting during the first week of its existence, as mentioned earlier. History, the fruit of the meetings, and the experience has proven one of the greatest revivals ever.

However, the localized revival of the Azusa movement did not stay confined at the mission. Later it was reported that Jennie Evans Moore, who was a member of First New Testament Church, spoke in tongues at the conclusion of the Easter morning service, April 15, 1906, causing quite a stir at that church. She quickly decided to attend Azusa regularly, and others soon followed.

The movement was like a wave that covered the earth and did so rapidly.[105] There were others during 1906 and 1907 that also received this experience. People in the British Islands, Norway, Denmark, Germany, Holland, Sweden, Russia, Bulgaria, Latvia, Finland, France, Italy, India, Central Africa, South Africa, Egypt, and South America.[106] The great experiences were being reported everywhere.

Arthur Osterberg, a converted Baptist, who reminisced about the first services at Azusa, claimed that some one hundred people were present while he attended. The Los Angeles Times reported a crowd that included mostly blacks with a few whites. In April 17, 1906, reporter Frank Bartleman visited the mission and said that there were approximately a dozen saints but that more people attended on weekends.

Most information says that there were about 300-500 worship attendees inside the forty-by-forty-foot whitewashed, wood-frame structure, with many people forced to stand outside the building before the end of the summer. They included seekers, hecklers, and children. Sometimes attendance may have exceeded 600-1000 attendees.

W.F. Manly reported in September of 1906 that there were twenty-five blacks and three hundred whites at the meetings he attended. What had occurred at Azusa began to spread quickly to other churches.

Some denominational churches were not open to the new revival and tongue talking and resisted the movement. A.H. Post, a Baptist pastor, tried to establish a Pentecostal work in Pasadena in July 1906, but he also experienced resistance.

6

Azusa Worshipers

Pictured: Frank Bartleman, Newspaper Reporter and Author.[182]

Frank Bartleman established a church on the corner of 8th and Maple in Los Angeles in August 1906. Seymour, the Lemons, and others from the Azusa mission held meetings in Whittier in August, September, and October of that year. One group held a Pentecostal meeting in the Holiness Church at Monrovia, California. Other ministers traveled north to Oakland, California and Salem,

Spokane, and Seattle, Washington. Still others like Abundio and Rosade Lopez moved southward to San Diego, California.

Initially, it appeared that the core of the mission's membership ran no more than fifty or sixty people. The official membership was racially integrated—although predominantly black—but whites mostly served in leadership positions. Seymour was black and so were his trustees Richard Asberry and James Alexander.

According to Osterberg's recorded and transcribed interview, his dad was a trustee in the beginning, but trust issues begin to arise with the whites and coloreds. He stated, the coloreds thought the whites were going to take over after questions arose about accounting of the finances. Osterberg said, they did not look at the color of people's faces. God was moving and that was all that mattered.

Seymour gave a verbal account of the money. His perspective was that it was God's money and he would give it out as God lead him. Some of the money was given for travel to Garr to go to India, and basic needs for the organization.

There was a unified team of responsible and post highly gifted black women such as Jennie Evans Moore, Lucy Farrow, and Ophelia Wiley who were joined by white women, Clara E. Lum and Florence Crawford, in public leadership roles. They led worship, read written testimonies, had leadership roles, and helped with the publication and distribution of The Apostolic Faith.

Seymour served as pastor of a congregation that did not fit the norm for the time. The church was a fully integrated work with leadership from blacks and whites, with Hispanics and other ethnic minorities comfortably present in most of the services.

Pictured: Five early Pentecostal leaders pictured at the Azusa Street Mission. In the front is the mission pastor, William J. Seymour, and John G. Lake; and standing from left to right are Brother Adams, F.F. Bosworth, and Tom Hezmalhalch[183]

Laboring men, working nearby, often spent their lunch period at the Azusa Mission. C.M. McGowan, a Methodist, got so interested he sometimes lost track of time. Later, his wife received her baptism in the Spirit, and God used her mightily in the Pentecostal circle and told other church groups about the baptism of the Holy Spirit.

Carlos P. Huntington, the wealthy railroad magnate, and his charming wife came in an elegant buggy, drawn by a well-groomed horse, to see this moving of God. Others came from all over the nation and from many parts of the world.

God used a stable in Los Angeles to open the floodgates of salvation and deliverance. Once a Methodist church and a horse stable, the Azusa Mission was now a pulpit for prophesying and preaching. Jesus was born in a stable. It is interesting how many great beginnings started in a stable.

The number of worshipers at Azusa was much larger than the core membership. The initial surge was in 1906-08, and the second one was in 1911. Only days before the second big surge, it was reported that there were as few as a dozen blacks and no whites. While the second rise was short-lived, it was sufficient to cause Bartleman to describe it as "the second shower of the latter reign." In 1912 an Anglican pastor and publisher of Confidence, A.A. Boddy, came from England and found a good-sized crowd though greatly reduced from that of the previous year.

Although Azusa was described by some as a "black" mission, the large crowds it attracted proved to be dominated by whites. Evangelists such as Gaston B. Cashwell, Frank Bartleman and "Mother" Elizabeth Wheaton came. Pastors Elmer Fisher, William Pendleton, William H. Durham, and Joseph S. Smale attended. Publishers such as Carrie Judd Montgomery and others also attended. M.L. Ryan (Apostolic Light), and A.S. Worrell (Gospel Witness) passed through and quickly spread the news. Veteran missionaries such as Samuel and Ardell Mead and Mae F. Mayo were there while church executives such as Charles H. Mason (Church of God in Christ) and Christian and Missionary Alliance District Superintendent George Eldridge attended. Some of them came for an extended period.

Most, but not all, seem to have come out of curiosity, though many came with the hope that they would receive something that they could take elsewhere—a new teaching.[107]

Pictured: Demos Shakerian.[184]

The Armenians established a Pentecostal church at 919 Boston Street, in the large home of Demos Shakarian, father of Isaac and grandfather of Demos, past president of the full Gospel Business Men's Fellowship International. The building still stands, and a continuation of this church is now at Goodrich and Carolina in east Los Angeles.[108]

About this time, Demos Shakarian and his brother-in-law, M. Mushagian, and another Armenian man, were strolling down San Pedro Street. As they neared Azusa, they heard familiar sounds, shouting and singing and praying similarly to what they were accustomed to in their own services. On reaching the Azusa Mission, they discovered several people speaking in tongues. They returned to their people with the thrilling news that God was beginning to move in America as he had in Armenia, in Russia, in the early churches, and in the upper room.

7

Views About Tongues and the Holy Spirit

The biblical basis for a Pentecostal theology of Spirit-baptism is sound. Pentecostalism interprets the baptism in "the Holy Spirit as the central doctrine of the Scriptures and the climax in the Christian life."[109]

The Pentecostal movement arose and grew in the United States in the early part of the twentieth century. The main emphasis was on the spectacular gift of the Holy Spirit. About the middle of the century, the Neo-Pentecostal or Charismatic movement began that had many of the same emphases. Pentecostal theology places greater emphasis on miracles, tongues, and healings than does Christianity in general.

Pentecostals make a theological explanation or basis for these healings and other manifestations of the Holy Spirit. When the question of the theological basis does come up, most Pentecostals often answer that these moves of the Spirit are found in atonement no less than forgiveness of sins, Baptism of the Holy Spirit, and salvation.

At the close of the nineteenth century when Charles Parham went to Topeka, Kansas, he found that his students focused on the topic of the baptism of the Holy Spirit. Some people in the class experienced the baptism of the Holy Spirit. This was, perhaps, the beginning of the modern Pentecostal movement. According to Millard J. Erickson, author of Christian Theology, the students' conclusion was that the Bible teaches that there is to be a baptism of the Holy Spirit after conversion and new birth and that speaking in tongues is the sign that one has received the gift.

According to Howard Ervin, author of Conversion Initiation and the Baptism in the Holy Spirit, says that, "He who was thus baptized in the Spirit, baptized, in turn, His disciples on the day of Pentecost. Jesus' experience of Spirit baptism does provide and unite all subsequent experiences of Spirit baptism with His in the history of salvation."

The Holy Spirit

The person of the Holy Spirit is important in Pentecostal theology. The Holy Spirit has occupied the center of the stage from the time of Pentecost on—that is, the period covered by the book of Acts and the epistles and the following periods of Church history.

To be in touch with God today, we must become acquainted with the Holy Spirit's activity. The Holy Spirit engages in moral actions and ministries that can be performed only by a person. These activities include more than just speaking in tongues—teaching, regenerating, searching, speaking, interceding, testifying, guiding, illuminating, and reveling. There are many gifts of the Spirit according 1 Corinthians 12.

The Pentecostals believed the following gifts were in operation today; the Holy Spirit and the gifts are for now. The Azusa outpourings focus was on glossolalia. In addition, the gifts of the Spirit were prevalent throughout the movement. According to the scripture below, 1 Corinthians 12 (MSG) Spiritual Gifts:

1-3 What I want to talk about now is the various ways God's Spirit gets worked into our lives. This is complex and often misunderstood, but I want you to be informed and knowledgeable. Remember how you were when you didn't know God, led from one phony god to another, never knowing what you were doing, just doing it because everybody else did it? It's different in this life. God wants us to use our intelligence, to seek to understand as well as we can. For instance, by using your heads, you know perfectly well that the Spirit of God would never prompt anyone to say, "Jesus be damned!" Nor would anyone be inclined to say, "Jesus is Master!" without the insight of the Holy Spirit.

4-11 God's various gifts are handed out everywhere; but they all originate in God's Spirit. God's various ministries are carried out everywhere; but they all originate in God's Spirit. God's various expressions of power are in action everywhere; but God himself is behind it all. Each person is given something to do that shows who God is: Everyone gets in on it, everyone benefits. All kinds of things are handed out by the Spirit, and to all kinds of people! The variety is wonderful: wise counsel, clear understanding, simple trust, healing the sick, miraculous acts, proclamation, distinguishing between spirits, tongues, interpretation of tongues. All these gifts have a common origin but are handed out one by one by the one Spirit of God. He decides who gets what, and when.

12-13 You can easily enough see how this kind of thing works by looking no further than your own body. Your body has many parts—limbs, organs, cells—but no matter how many parts you can name, you're still one body. It's exactly the same with Christ. By means of His one Spirit, we all said good-bye to our partial and piecemeal lives. We each used to independently call our own shots, but then we entered into a large and integrated life in which he has the final say in everything. (This is what we proclaimed in word and action when we were baptized.) Each of us is now a part of His resurrection body, refreshed and sustained at one fountain—His Spirit—where we all come to drink. The old labels we once used to identify ourselves—labels like Jew or Greek, slave or free—are no longer useful. We need something larger, more comprehensive.

14-18 I want you to think about how all this makes you more significant, not less. A body isn't just a single part blown up into something huge. It's all the different-but-similar parts arranged and functioning together. If Foot said, "I'm not elegant like Hand, embellished with rings; I guess I don't belong to this body," would that make it so? If Ear said, "I'm not beautiful like Eye, limpid and expressive; I don't deserve a place on the head," would you want to remove it from the body? If the body was all eye, how could it hear? If all ear, how could it smell? As it is, we see that God has carefully placed each part of the body right where he wanted it.

19-24 But I also want you to think about how this keeps your significance from getting blown up into self-importance. For no matter how significant you are, it is only because of what you are a part of. An enormous eye or a gigantic hand wouldn't be a body, but a monster. What we have is one body with many parts, each its proper size and in its proper place. No part is important on its own. Can you imagine Eye telling Hand, "Get lost; I don't need you"? Or, Head telling Foot, "You're fired; your job has been phased out"? As a matter of fact, in practice it works the other way—the "lower" the part, the more basic, and therefore necessary. You can live without an eye, for instance, but not without a stomach. When it's a part of your own body you are concerned with, it makes no difference whether the part is visible or clothed, higher or lower. You give it dignity and honor just as it is, without comparisons. If anything, you have more concern for the lower parts than the higher. If you had to choose, wouldn't you prefer good digestion to full-bodied hair?

25-26 The way God designed our bodies is a model for understanding our lives together as a church: every part dependent on every other part, the parts we mention and the parts we don't, the parts we see and the parts we don't. If one-part hurts, every other part is involved in the hurt, and in the healing. If one-part flourishes, every other part enters into the exuberance.

27-31 You are Christ's body—that's who you are! You must never forget this. Only as you accept your part of that body does your "part" mean anything. You're familiar with some of the parts that God has formed in His church, which is His "body": Apostles, prophets, teachers, miracle workers, healers, helpers, organizers, those who pray in tongues.

But it's obvious by now, isn't it, that Christ's church is a complete Body and not a gigantic, unidimensional Part? It's not all Apostle, not all Prophet, not all Miracle Worker, not all Healer, not all Prayer in Tongues, not all Interpreter of Tongues. And yet some of you keep competing for so-called "important" parts.

But now I want to lay out a far better way for you."

The Spirit gave prophecy and Scripture.[110] Another work of the Spirit of God in the Old Testament was in conveying certain necessary skills for various tasks.[111]

There are, however, some cases where the New Testament makes it clear that an Old Testament reference to the "Spirit of God" is a reference to the Holy Spirit. Acts 2:16-21 is a prominent New Testament passage; Peter explains that what is occurring at Pentecost is the fulfillment of the prophet Joel's statement, "I will pour out my Spirit upon all flesh." Surely the events of Pentecost were the realization of Jesus' promise: "You shall receive power when the Holy Spirit has come upon you" (Acts 1:8). In short, the Old Testament "Spirit of God" is synonymous with the Holy Spirit.[112]

Jesus and the Holy Spirit

When we examine Jesus' life, we find a persuasive and powerful presence of the Spirit throughout.[113] Even the very beginning of His incarnate existence was a work of the Holy Spirit, both the prediction and the records of the birth of Jesus point to a special working of the Spirit.[114]

The Holy Spirit conceived Jesus—that is, His physical birth was by the direct action of the Holy Spirit. He was the incarnation of the Word of God. By the Holy Spirit's action, God's only Son—the Creative Word, who existed for all eternity with the Father, and by whom the world was created—took on a human soul and body. When He did this, He set aside His power and temporarily accepted the limitations of natural humanity (Phil. 2:7-8).[115]

The Holy Spirit is evident from the very beginning of Jesus' public ministry. The Holy Spirit came upon Him in the form of a dove (Matthew 3:16, Mark 1:10, Luke 3:22, and John 1:32). Matthew and Mark did not say that Jesus saw the descending dove; they do not tell us whether anyone else did. Luke does not record who saw the dove. Only John makes clear that John the Baptist also saw the Spirit and bore witness to the fact. None of the accounts mention any particular manifestations or visible effects or something similar. We do know, however, that immediately afterward, Jesus was "full of the Holy Spirit" (Luke 4:1). The Holy Spirit operated in Jesus life throughout His ministry.

Jesus' Emphasis on the Work of the Holy Spirit

In Jesus' teaching we find an especially strong emphasis upon the work of the Holy Spirit in initiating people into the Christian life. Jesus makes it clear to Nicodemus that regeneration is miraculous transformation of the individual and impartation of spiritual power essential to acceptance by the Father. Jesus makes reference in the Scripture that regeneration is a supernatural occurrence, and the Holy Spirit is the agent who produces it.[116]

Jesus states in the Word that the Holy Spirit would indwell and illuminate the believer.
> And I will pray the Father, and He will give you another
> Counselor, to be with you forever, the Spirit of truth,
> who the world cannot receive, because it neither sees
> Him nor knows Him. You know Him, for He dwells with
> you, and will be in you. (John 14: 16-17)

Another point of particular interest is the intercessory work of the Holy Spirit. The Holy Spirit also works sanctification in the life of believers, and that is a progressive work.

Azusa and the Holy Spirit

During the Azusa outpouring, sanctification was taking place in the people. This was an important part of the movement. The Spirit also bestowed certain gifts upon believers—those who lived sanctified and set apart lives. Throughout the Azusa Mission there were reports of miraculous gifts. Most of the gifts that were reported were gifts of faith, healing, exorcism of demons, and especially glossolalia.

The Holy Spirit dispenses these gifts in the Church today. These same gifts have been evident in both denominational and interdenominational churches. However, it seems that the gifts are more prevalent in interdenominational settings. "There is no indication that the Holy Spirit would cease to bestow this gift on the Church."[117] Pentecostals, as they are known today are Christians that sought a deeper blessing. One of these blessing is speaking in tongues.[118]

Tongues and Interpretation

The gifts of utterance, tongues, interpretation, and prophecy, are not solely to guide our lives but to help reveal God to us and to help us in our response to Him. God manifested two ways of speaking in tongues. One way was as a devotional language for private information, needing no interpretation. The other way was through tongues and interpretation.

The reports mentioned about Azusa in 1906, show that people also spoke in tongues during the service. They would sing in tongues, pray in tongues, and some were on the floor speaking in a language that no one understood. There were those who interpreted the song or message in English. Speaking in tongues was also used as a devotional or a prayer to God among Christians.

Often an experiential argument is employed to emphasize the benefits that tongues produces in the Christian's spiritual life, especially its value for vitalizing one's prayer life.[119] Speaking to God in other tongues has been very beneficial in Christian's lives.

Have Gifts Ceased?

Some reject the idea that the Holy Spirit is still dispensing the charismatic gifts. They argue that the miraculous gifts ceased. They were virtually unknown throughout most of the history of the Church.[120]

Some people argue that God did not intend to give tongues, unlike prophecy and knowledge, until the end times. Tongues are not included concerning the imperfect gifts that will pass away when the perfect come.[121] They say that the miraculous signs were to validate the revelation of Jesus as God's son, and that once they had fulfilled that purpose those signs simply faded away.[122]

According to P. Feene, Speaking with Tongues is looked at from the perspective that glossolalia or tongues are not to be interpreted as special gifts of the Holy Spirit. An example is the Church of Corinth. The church in Corinth had ecstatic utterances not unlike Pentecostalism's tongues.[123]

Those who believe the gifts have ceased cite psychological studies that find parallels between speaking in tongues and certain cases of heightened suggestibility such as by brainwashing or shock.[124]

Linguists have also attempted to study glossolalia, finding mixed results. Those who believe that tongues represents existing human languages must answer scientific charges that state many cases of glossolalia simply do not display several characteristics of language.[125]

Another argument centers on the study of the baptism of the Holy Spirit. The book of Acts, which speaks of a special work of the Spirit after the new birth, covers a transitional period. Many Christians are converted and regenerated. Some questions may be asked: What about the clear separation between conversion and regeneration and the baptism of the Spirit?

Tongues in Acts involved people who were regenerated before they received the Holy Spirit. They were the last of the Old Testament believers.[126] They had not received the Spirit before the events of Pentecost; however, because He could not be revealed until Jesus had ascended.[127] The disciples were already regenerated under the New Testament system but were not filled until the day of Pentecost. The Bible teaches that the Spirit dispenses special gifts today. According to 1 Corinthians 12:11, He bestows them sovereignly; He alone decides the recipients. If He chooses to give us a special gift, He can do so despite whether we expect it or seek it. According to Ephesians 5:15, we are commanded to be filled with the Holy Spirit. This is a present imperative, suggesting ongoing action. According to Ervin, the final use of the phrase "filled with the Spirit" is found in Ephesians 5:18, which says, "And do not get drunk with wine, for that is debauchery, but be filled with the Spirit." In this text, the word for "be filled," means either continuous or repeated action.[128]

When Azusa was in full swing, the Holy Spirit's move was phenomenal. The Holy Spirit bestowed the gifts upon the attendees regularly. This was not Seymour's own accomplishment but was to be used in the fulfillment of God's plan. God dispensed His gifts to the Church wisely and with His sovereign might—they were not rewards for those who "qualified."

The Holy Spirit regenerates men. The action of the Spirit helps to organize people into Himself as the living center. The head and the body are therefore one and predestined to be the same history of humiliation and glory.[129] James Dunn, author of *Baptism in the Holy Spirit*, says that there is one Body and one Spirit. He states, "We can say that Pentecost is the beginning of the Church and the coming into existence of the church as the Body of Christ."[130] Dunn says there were no "Christians" before Pentecost. However, the disciples were closely identified with Jesus until their first recognition in Acts 11:26 when they were called Christians first in Antioch.

The Pentecostal interpretation of the baptism in the Holy Spirit is that it occurs after conversion and the new birth. Dunn states that it happens at the same time as conversion and the new birth. Luke does not speak of the Gift of the Spirit in association with the New Birth. Dunn argues that the disciples were born again at the time of the resurrection and argues that this is not Luke's view.[131] The Holy Spirit's mission first started out in Jesus' disciples.

Clearly, under the New Covenant, the work of the Spirit involves an internal change, although theologians have debated when and how the Spirit enters a person's life.[132] There is still certain hope because of the living Christ, dwelling within as our personal "hope of glory" (Colossians 1:27).[133]

Moves of Pentecost and tongues of fire have been prominent occurrences throughout the History of the Church. The Book of Acts is the first book of Church history. It gives us the highlights in the story of Christianity during A. D. 30-60, that is, during the first generation.

It is an important document because the spread of Christianity has been the most significant movement in the last two thousand years.[134] The beginning of the Church at Pentecost expounded upon Jesus' promise. The Holy Spirit had been with them (par'humin) while Jesus was on earth. After Jesus was resurrected, the

Holy Spirit would be *in* them (en humin).[135] While Pentecost took place; thousands were attracted to faith in Jesus.

The Holy Spirit marked a new era. The Church grew vastly in Judea, Samaria, and the other parts of the world. Gentiles even received salvation, and nothing could stop the moving of the Spirit.[136]

The Azusa outpouring of 1906 has made the spread of Christianity a second part of the greatest manifestation of the Holy Spirit's Pentecostal influence that history has known. The Holy Spirit has always been the agent in accomplishing God's purpose from the time of prophets, the epoch of Jesus' ministry, and the era of the Church's mission.[137]

Some great men of our time have known the "secret power" of the Holy Spirit. Seymour affected many. After receiving the baptism of the Holy Spirit, God moved him into powerful meetings, and He stirred the faith of thousands to receive healing and salvation through His servant Seymour.[138]

B.H. Irwin, who in the 1880s provided the doctrinal bridge between Holiness and Pentecostal churches and preached that the reception of the Holy Spirit and fire came after sanctification. Irwin did not preach that speaking in tongues was the sign of having received the Holy Spirit, but "this phenomenon was quite common among those who received the fire."[139] Irwin's doctrine spread rapidly, and his congregation expanded. The Holiness churches reflected this theological change.[140] He began the biblical basis for the theological thrust of the Pentecostal movement.[141]

The religious leaders said Jesus did not act normally in Mark 3:21 and accused Him of having a devil. During Pentecost, people accused the disciples of being drunk (Acts 2:13). Many thought Paul was mad (Acts 23:24). These were great men of God whom the world said were crazed. God used them, and the Spirit dwelled within their bodies and made them drunk.[142]

Organizational Lines

By 1920, much of the theological excitement had subsided, and most of the organizational lines of the movement were set, although divisions proceeded on a smaller scale. The southern churches maintained their earlier doctrinal beliefs. The positions remained particularly Trinitarian and Wesleyan about sanctification. It was also said that the various doctrinal differences were outweighed by the basic similarities in beliefs and practice. The southern churches—including the non-holiness denominations—stressed an evangelical view.

The Holiness Pentecostal movement began as a broad-based movement. By the 1920s, Pentecostalism was restricted predominantly to the lower classes. This was especially true in blacks and accounts for part of the large differences between the rural immigrants and blacks of the northern cities. The migrating blacks were not at home in northern black churches.

Government figures reflect that during 1926 and 1936, what was characterized as regular churches lost 2,000,000 members (eight percent of their total). The Holiness and Pentecostal movement's churches grew rapidly.[143] The Pentecostal Assemblies increased 264%, the Assemblies of God 208%, the Church of the Nazarene 114%, the Church of God 92%, and the Pentecostal Holiness Church 60%.[144]

The Church today needs the power that is associated with the New Testament teachings. When we focus totally on the New Testament teaching, the Church will have a Pentecostal experience that the world will not forget.

In the early part of 1967, the Catholic Church began to have Pentecostal experiences that were termed the "Charismatic movement."[145] Approximately five years later, it was the most talked about movement within the Church.[146] This emphasis was based upon the New Testament teachings and charismatic experiences that were prevalent throughout. Apostle Paul taught on the central theme of the New Testament, and the Holy Spirit was part of his major message.[147]

The Pentecostals have a distinctive theology, and a great portion of this theology is from the modern Pentecostal movement, which emphasized the ministry of the Spirit. Pentecostalism has shown a strong allegiance to the mainstream theology.[148] In this sense, nothing really new has been added to the Church; God has merely recalled her to the beliefs of the first Christians.[149] The humility of the people on Azusa Street gave cohesiveness to the great revival that became known as the modern Pentecostal movement.[150] They let God work through them to change history.

God used Charles F. Parham and William J. Seymour and the Pentecostal experience of 1901 (and 1906) to increase the understanding of spirit-manifestations, particularly speaking in tongues. They made a connection between the baptism in the Spirit and speaking in other tongues or glossolalia.[151] Since the birth of the modern Pentecostal movement, tongues has been the theological affirmation that gave identity and continuity to the revival.[152]

Pentecostal Churches

Classical Pentecostalism was prevalent during the turn of the century.[153] The Church had expanded relevantly throughout the world—especially Latin America and the Third World.[154]

They thought of the gifts of the Spirit and the baptism in the Spirit as a second blessing with the evidence of tongues.[155] The older churches did not operate in the fullness of the experience of the Holy Spirit, and they went on without operating in the New Testament gifts.[156] For decades, other churches and theologians generally saw nothing more than a modern upsurge of long familiar forms of enthusiasm in Pentecostalism.

Some Church leaders and Christians did not believe that spiritual gifts were from God. Some of the Baptist, Methodist, Presbyterian churches were not fond of the healing and Pentecostal revival. They believed in a cessation theology, meaning healing and the gifts of the Spirit were not for today. They said that they were "demonically inspired delusion than merely excessive zeal and misguided exegesis."[157] Today, there is more of a wide spread acceptance to the baptism of the Spirit, but the Church still has a way to go.

The Assemblies of God, a church fellowship, traces its origins to the Pentecostal outpouring. Some preachers who started the movement were put out or not welcomed in their previous churches after such a great awakening. These ministers began to speak of this great experience—the initial physical evidence of the baptism in the Spirit. This experience was vastly growing and was understood as an anointing for service, and not a badge of sanctification.

Aimee Semple McPherson directed the Foursquare Church. She was widely known and helped people to start great works of God. McPherson's financial blessings helped one of the original Azusa members, Mother Emma Cotton, to purchase the old Azusa Mission church in the 1920's.

Dr. Gwyneth Williams & Star Williams

Pictured: Fifty Year Golden Jubilee Celebration of the 1906 Azusa Revival.[185]

McPherson did not help with the 50th year anniversary of the Azusa Street Mission, because of her death in 1944. This event was called the Golden Jubilee. It was held at Angelus Temple, located in Los Angeles, California, in 1956.

McPherson founded the Foursquare Church based on what she called the "Foursquare Message." The inspiration for the church came while she was in Oakland, California during July 1922.

Another church affected by the baptism of the Holy Spirit was the Church of God in Cleveland, Tennessee. This church was started when people from Tennessee [158] and North Carolina felt an urge to seek God on a deeper level.[159] The people wanted a new experience. As a result, the people received the baptism in the Holy Spirit. It was reported that in 1896 there were approximately 100 people filled with the Holy Spirit who spoke with other tongues.[160] Over the years, this church has experienced many periods of growth.

Some older churches were questionable regarding the Pentecostal experience. The experience of Pentecost was an example of what God can do today. "The churches had too long forgotten, indeed repressed, that Christian life is in the spirit, and ought by its very nature to display manifest signs of its transforming and invigorating energy."[161]

Christianity Today

The Christian Church can set a new pace for today's world. The world needs Christ today as never before. Our teenagers worship idols and paganism is on the rise. "There is a need for the same supernatural power of the Apostolic days."[162] The Church must totally put her trust in God if she wants to receive the blessings that God has for her. The Church is in bad shape and needs a more innate communion with God. The Pentecostal blessings will shower us with power for

God. There is no reason for the Church to get into "the fleshly extravagances prevalent among some Christian people."[163]

The Church should put its eyes upon Scriptural truth rather than on people who imperfectly try to put Scriptural truth into action. Man ought to seek the face of God for what God has for him. We should note that revival today has some peculiar marks about it.[164] Revival has always borne many peculiar marks. These marks are not unlike certain marks found in the Book of Acts and in Paul's Epistles.

Revival always comes from God working through someone who is willing to carry out the functions to which no one else is willing to yield him or herself.[165] God is looking for humble men and women who will preach the truth of the Gospel without compromise.[166]

8

The Charismatic and Pentecostal Church Today

The history of the Pentecostal and Charismatic movement goes back to the Azusa Street mission.[167] We cannot look at Church history and Pentecostalism without reflecting on these great events that happened in the United States and covered the world. Every Pentecostal church can trace its roots back to the great outpouring of 1906.[168] To understand our churches today, particularly the Pentecostal and Charismatic churches, we must understand the movement. It will help us understand our purpose and focus according to the Word and from a historical perspective.

Tongues had an effect on churches and caused many questions and some disturbances in more traditional churches. Many churches did not want to accept this new and strange doctrine.

Today, the Pentecostal and Charismatic churches are growing rapidly. Many storefront churches have sprung from the movement.

According to Bishop Lesslie Newbigin, during the 1960's the Pentecostal movement grew rapidly: "A grass edge can be untidy for two reasons: because it is neglected, or because it is growing." Bishop Newbigin was unmistakably referring to the Pentecostal Movement.[169] The growth has been phenomenal, and some upkeep has been neglected.

Pentecostalism has flourished into the world's fastest growing denomination at a time when membership in most other churches are declining.[170] It bears repeating that this event was one of the most power packed events that the Church has known.[171] Vinson Synan states, "There are over 200,000,000 classical Pentecostals in uncounted churches and missions in the world.[172] There are 430,000,000, Pentecostals and Charismatics in every denomination who can trace at least part of their spiritual heritage to the Azusa Street meetings."[173] A study done in 2011, estimates 279 million classical Pentecostals. Since 1906 close to one billion people living and dead have been affected by this great outpouring.

The Charismatic movement is using the gift of faith. Charismatic churches are usually involved in social functions and politics. Many Charismatic churches have experienced growth spurts in short periods. The point John Wesley himself once prayed, "But if this cannot be, send it—with all its defects. We must have revival in America" after the revival of his day had nearly died out for the time.

The Church today can have what it has had in the past. She still has the gifts of the Holy Spirit flowing. The church today presents a balanced picture of tongues and the gifts of the Holy Spirit. Also, the Pentecostal theology is balanced and there is some conformity to 1 Corinthians chapters 12, 13, and 14.[174]

Results of the Pentecostal and Charismatic Movements

The results of the Charismatic and Pentecostal Church movements can bring forth a revival to further the Great Commission. Jesus said, "On this rock I will build my church, and the gates of Hades will not overcome it" Matthew 16:18. God has selected the Church as a body of disciples that will help carry out His plans. God wants to see all nationalities walking together in love and accepting the Holy Spirit as their focus.

God's Word gives us instructions on how to carry out His plans. He said "Go, therefore, and make disciples of all nations, baptizing them in the name of the Father and of the Son and of the Holy Spirit, teaching them to observe whatsoever I have commanded you" (Matthew 28:19-20).

There has been continual growth since the inception of the Charismatic and Pentecostal movement. The results reflect healthy and vigorous expansion in the past years along with the major influences the Church has had on the community and the unchurched throughout the world. God's hand is on the Charismatics, the Classical Pentecostals, and the Pentecostal Church.

Pictured: Last known picture of William J. Seymour.[186]

Moving With the Spirit

One reason God found the people of Azusa so easy to move through was their experience. They were not novices, and in fact many had felt called for years. God had been preparing them and drew them from the Holiness ranks and from the mission field, etc. They had been tried and proven. They were largely seasoned veterans. They were pioneers, shock troops like Gideon's three hundred gathered to spread the fire around the world. The Spirit moved among the people because of their thirst and hunger for God's approval. The flesh could not glorify itself at Azusa. The manifestation of the Lord was great among the meetings. The people wanted a touch from God, and they wanted to enter the Throne of Grace.

In the period surrounding the Azusa outpouring, people sought the Lord for days and hours, examining their minds, wills, and emotions. Azusa was important and inspired others to come and receive the conversion experience. People could not totally understand the spiritual events, but their finite minds yielded to the things of the Spirit. Many found their intellectual orientation transformed. The direction and guidance that the people needed was there. God had them there for new beginnings, and His Church grew in power, strength, and number because of the yielded vessels at Azusa. It set the stage for the work of modern, spirit filled missions today.

The Church has been endowed with the power of the Holy Spirit. Jesus commanded us to make disciples of all nations—not only Jews but Samaritans and Gentiles (Matt. 28:19, 20). After the coming of the Holy Spirit upon them, the Apostles became Christ's witnesses not only in Jerusalem and Judea but in Samaria and to the ends of the earth (Acts 1:8).

The Next Generation

There are groups that have come about later. The main focus of these groups are the gifts of the Spirit. Vineyard Fellowship of Churches founded by John Wimber. Then there arose the "Toronto Blessing" with John and Carol Arnott. Others included C. Peter Wagner.

Statistician David Barrett stated these waves of revival to be "one single cohesive movement into which a vast proliferation of all kinds of individuals and communities have been drawn. Whether termed Pentecostals, Charismatics or Third Wave, they share a basic, single experience. Their contribution to Christianity is a new awareness of Spiritual gifts as a ministry to the life of the Church."

The Modern Pentecostal Charismatic Movement is dynamic and the fastest growing movement in the world. The movement is growing at a rate of 25 million per year. Two-thirds of all populations in developing nations once known as third world, identify themselves as Pentecostal charismatics. The movement is found among eight thousand different ethnic groups who speak seven thousand different languages.

The 100 Year Prophecy:

One hundred years ago, William J. Seymour, the leader of the Azusa Street Revival and Charles Parham both prophesied on the same day in different locations that we would see a Greater Revival in 100 years. They said, "We are not yet up to the fullness of the Former Rain and that when the Latter Rain comes, it will far exceed anything we have seen. The 100 years there would be an outpouring of God's Spirit and His Shekinah Glory that would be greater and more far reaching than what was expected at Azusa."

"The roots of the modern-day outpouring of the Spirit can be traced to a clapboard building during the turn-of-the-century in Los Angeles, California. The revival that took place at the Azusa Street Mission from 1906 to 1919 sparked the remarkable worldwide growth of the Pentecostal movement and its sister, the Charismatic renewal. Although this revival is significant for a number of reasons, the most important lesson of Azusa Street for this current generation is the power of spiritual unity."

> "And it shall come to pass afterward That I will pour out My Spirit on all flesh; Your sons and your daughters shall prophesy, Your old men shall dream dreams, Your young men shall see visions. And also, on My menservants and on My maidservants I will pour out My Spirit in those days." Joel 2:28-29

9

Azusa Now

China 1986

Ambassador Gwyneth and the team visited state churches and were introduced to many government officials. The team took suitcases of Bibles wrapped in Christmas papers. They were told if asked they were gifts. It was with great honor to be with Nora Lam, Ralph Wilkerson, Arthur Blessitt and others. Blessitt carries the cross around the world and now on the Great Wall of China in a communist country. The first night the team gathered, it was with great joy for Ambassador Gwyneth to receive one of his Jesus stickers.

Lam an American citizen later had a movie produced about her titled, "China Cry." She grew up in China and was hosting the team. She planned for Blessitt to walk through China. According to Blessitt, Lam did not tell anyone that he was 'walking with a cross.' The news media was there to welcome the 'world's greatest walker' not Blessitt who walked with the cross. The media wanted Blessitt to pose for the newspaper without the cross, but he did not lay down the cross.

The team was so excited when the cross was screwed together. Blessitt lifted it up and carried it on his shoulders and started up the steps of the Great Wall of China. Ambassador Gwyneth climbed following the cross praying and making proclamations. When everyone reached the top. The cross was lifted on the Great Wall of China. There was a shift in the atmosphere.

When she arrived at the top of the steps, she knew this was a great victory. This was an historic moment for Ambassador Gwyneth, the team, and China. The view from the top was magnificent. What a wonderful day for her and a time she would cherish for a lifetime. Prayer mapping, praying in a communist nation, and being with these awesome legends.

Ambassador Gwyneth was in awe when she was walking on the Great Wall of China as everyone took one step at a time. Blessitt continued to carry the cross on the wall. What a historic moment seeing this with Lam. The power of Christ, Pentecost, Prayer Mapping and believing for a greater awakening in China. It was a glorious moment.

Blessitt said, "The glory of God was sweeping over me and excitement filled my

body. This is the heart of communist China! This was the cross for Jesus being lifted up where few ever thought it could happen."

In a country that is home for over a billion people, the big 12-foot cross was now on top of the Great Wall of China. The report and photos went around the world via the news media. Overnight the officials of the country had grace and they were not sent out of the country with the cross!

According to history and Blessitt's journal, the cross is being carried openly in Red China. This was the first public manifestation of Christianity and religion in modern China in over forty years.

Not since Mao Tse Tung, and later the Gang of Four tried to destroy Christianity. This land once swept with the blood of martyrs is now having the cross openly carried through the countryside and the cities. Mao Tse Tung must be rolling over in his grave!

In 1986 for 40 years most people had not heard the Gospel. The Azusa Street Outpouring and Pentecost in China was ripe for harvest. There are multitudes of people in China waiting to hear and receive the word of God.

During this time the only people who had vans were business owners. Early mornings as Ambassador Gwyneth would look out the window there were thousands of bicycles. There did not seem to be a system or traffic lights. Everyone was riding, and it seemed they were going as fast as they could and in all directions. People who fell off their bicycles or were knocked off got up fast and continued on in high speed. During the day on the streets were hundreds of bikes parked. Ambassador Gwyneth wondered how they could identify them, but some of them had a number on the bicycles.

In the mainland China you are never alone. There are so many people waiting for an outpouring. The team took a passenger ride on a train through the country side. Ambassador Gwyneth could see Chinese men working with small chisels taking down brick structures brick by brick. This is how we can reach each soul, one soul at a time. The Chinese must ultimately win China to Christ. God will use them to inspire, to preach and teach one another.

Testimonies in China

- Many of the team members went to different locations. Ambassador Gwyneth went to the house church. They were able to share the gospel. One of the men, through the interpreter, Lam's son, said they were afraid to say much because they thought there may be informants in the meeting.
- During one of the outings Ambassador Gwyneth was able to pass out a gospel tract to a communist soldier. He was a young soldier. The Lord instructed her to get off the bus and hand it to him. When she got back on she looked out the window and he was reading it. In addition, she left tracts in different locations. Many seeds of the Gospel planted.
- Blessitt, stated he went with a man named Benji who was a Chinese Christian. He witnessed to the eager young people who were searching for Jesus. He led one girl to Jesus. She said, "Do you have to speak English to speak with Jesus?"
- Someone asked, "Will Jesus come into a Chinese heart?" "Yes," Benji said, "I am Chinese."

- Benji told a young girl about 20 years old with eyes alive, emotions overflowing as Benji tried to interpret she asked, "Was this like the cross Jesus died on?" She was a believer, a Christian and she was so excited she wanted us to come to her House-Church.
- Blessitt, let one of the first Chinese men carry the cross.

The Great Wall of China stretches for thousands of miles across the vast country. It has been known for more than two thousand years as one of the great wonders of the world. China is old it has five thousand years of history. What a blessing for Ambassador Gwyneth to be on the Great Wall of China going into this new year.

Now she has entered 1987. China celebrated on New Year's at midnight. When time approached the city absolutely exploded. There were explosions by the hundreds. Everything was lite up. A great celebration with everyone sending rockets into the air.

When Ambassador Gwyneth left China, she was filled with a sense of what God wanted her to experience was accomplished. When she was 16 she had an open vision while praying on her knees at a Tuesday night prayer meeting. She saw herself going to China and a young Chinese girl's face came before her. The girl asked her to come to China. A few months later a young man came to church and prophesied that Ambassador Gwyneth would travel around the world. This was that prophesied by the Prophet Joel, "I will pour out my Spirit on all people. Your sons and daughters will prophecy. Your old men will dream dreams, and your young men will see visions." Joel 2:28

Again, what an awesome time in history to see the continuation of the Baptism of the Holy Spirit at work and the Azusa Legacy continue through Ambassador Gwyneth. Many tracks passed out, witnessing to the communist soldier, prayer mapping and the miracle, the girl she saw in the open vision was there in the house church. Through an interpreter she was able to share the vision of seeing her years ago. The completion and reason for her being there was to plant the seeds of the Gospel of Jesus Christ and to learn from these great legends Nora Lam, Arthur Blessitt, and Ralph Wilkerson.

Since then she has returned on three occasions, reminding the Christians of the hope and the Azusa Outpouring.

Bahamas, Andros Island 1987 and 1989

One of the first open air meetings outside the United States of America Ambassador Gwyneth did was on the Island of Andros. People heard the gospel from door to door outreach. Many people were baptized with the Holy Spirit, there were healings, Ambassador Gwyneth prayed for a woman who went through deliverance. She vomited up a large amount of white creamy substance. Hundreds

of children gave their lives to the Lord in the schools. Wedding vows renewed. The team totaled 7 and 10 on the next team in 1989, she trained them. Also, all team members were baptized with the Holy Spirit and there was a great impartation on the Island.

Jamaica 1990, 1993, and 2010

Taken three teams. Training, outreaches, ministry in the orphanage, and Youth seminars. Ministry and Teaching on the Baptism of the Holy Spirit and holiness. Numerous people were touched. Clark laid hands on hundreds of people with V.T. Williams, Ambassadors Gwyneth and Star as they prayed for people who received the Azusa impartation. People received the Baptism with the Holy Spirit and Fire. Also, some received a refreshing.

Mexico 1990 and 2000

Five teams to Mexico. Carrying the fire of the Holy Spirit. Outreach to those living in adverse cases. Adults and children living in card board boxes. Teams ministered in outreaches, orphanages, to students, and brought supplies. The teams were a part of great outreaches throughout the country. Many souls were Baptized with the Holy Spirit

England 1987, 1988, 1998, 2011, 2014, 2015

Worked with Wynne Lewis and Colin Dye. Bishop Otis Clark did an impartation of the fire of the Holy Spirit at Ruach Ministries. Clark at the age of 108 laid hands on 2,500 individuals for the Azusa impartation. Worked with youth, outreach to Muslims, women's ministry amongst the white British, lived in the culture one year studying, research and writing. Taken healing teams of 35 to release the fire of the Holy Spirit. Much ground has been tilled in England.

France 1987, 1988, 2015

Taken teams to France for street evangelism and Prophetic prayer mapping.

Zimbabwe, Africa 2006, 2007

Bishop Otis, Ambassadors Gwyneth and Star took three teams. These were historical events of the outreaches, open air meetings, youth, women, and leaders. Ministry in the villages; and schools reaching thousands of students with the gospel.

Bishop Otis Clark

Dad was a man of adventure. He traveled the roads of America since 1921. In the 1930's, he sold his 1929 Nash to make a trip to Africa on which he did not get to go. Dad was well known for driving from Tulsa, Oklahoma to California without stopping to sleep with his trusty bag of Fritos. The Fritos helped him stay awake while driving. He believed there was a connection between your taste buds and mental alertness. Dad's last trip by himself to California was in 2001 when he was 98 years old. He drove to San Francisco to bury his nephew Robert. On this last trip to California, Dad "swung" by Seattle, Washington to unsuccessfully apply for a passport. On the road trips he'd rarely stop to sleep, unless it was for a few minutes at a rest stop. Dad enjoyed seeing the sights of the road, including the trees and the different landscapes. One of his main memories was going from gravel roads to paved highways.

Dad, A World Traveler

His idea of living was traveling around the world blessing people with the love of God. The spirit of Dad was free, independent and unencumbered. His life and joy came from traveling, rather driving, flying, or sailing. He lit up at the idea of going somewhere.

Despite his unsuccessful attempt to go to Africa in the 1930's, he made it in 2006 at the young age of 103 and returned for a second time in 2007 at the age of 104. He was a go-getter. When asked if he was tired or needed some rest, and he'd reply, "Tired? Tired of doing what?!" To Dad, ministry was his life source, and he did not view it as work, but living. He loved to travel and always said that God called him as an evangelist. God knew what He was doing when He called him to be an evangelist. Dad was the oldest traveling evangelist in the world, amongst many other things.

While in Africa, Dad touched many lives for Christ. He loved people and shared Christ everywhere he went. "If you're on God's side you're a winner…" was his famous saying, and he shared it everywhere he went, "If you're on God's side, you're a winner. If you're not on God's side, you are a loser. Get on God's side!"

His message carried simplicity and profoundness. Revelations 3:15-16 reinforces Dad's legendary words—"I know your deeds, that you are neither cold nor hot. I wish you were either one or the other! So, because you are lukewarm—neither hot nor cold—I am about to spit you out of my mouth. Everyone must choose a side to be on—God's or Satan's side, the choice belongs to each individual.

Azusa Street Outpouring

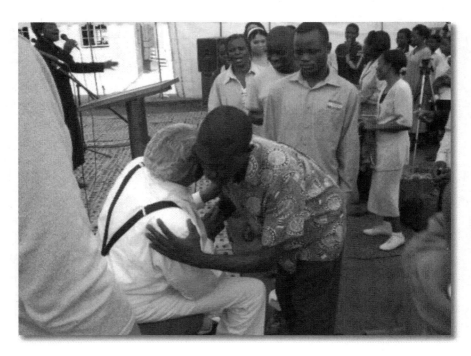

Bishop Clark ministering to those infected with AIDS and laying hands on every participant at the tent revival Zimbabwe, Africa,

When Bishop Otis Clark went to heaven and was promoted to his eternal home he told his daughter and granddaughter to continue the legacy. They are continuing his legacy. His life and legacy have left a mark that cannot be erased and only continues to grow.

They are the descendants of Clark, who was known as one of the last living witnesses of the Azusa Street Revival. They are taking it to the nations what was passed on to them; the actual Power-of-Attorney and Prophetic Baton from the original Azusa International Mission.

Clark's assignment was to continue the legacy of the Azusa International Mission. For Over 90 years he faithfully carried the torch, fire, and power of the Holy Spirit around the world until the age of 109 years young. He preached on a Sunday and went home to be with the Lord on the Monday before Pentecost 2012.

Before he left, he mandated and passed the Power-of-Attorney to them, to carry on as the next generation, the mantle of signs, wonders, miracles, and healings; unleashing the Holy Spirit and making room for Him to have His way. They are contending for an awakening and releasing the Azusa Apostolic Faith Impartation of the Holy Spirit. In ministries, homes, and businesses coast to coast and around the world.

Canada 2008, 2010, 2012

Releasing the fire of revival. Bishop Otis, Ambassadors Gwyneth, and Star Traveled on 4 occasions ministering in public schools; churches; the mayor's office; newspaper interview; national live television; and on Bay Street (Canada's Wall Street) preaching the gospel of Jesus Christ. Touching government, media, family, education, business, and many aspects of society. In the school they spoke on the subject of Overcoming Rejection to live, dream and hope again;

forgiveness and reconciliation. Preventing bullying and school violence. Giving hope to the First Nations people. They've Ministered in the provinces of Ontario, British Columbia and Alberta.

Azusa Now 2013-2015

Marked by signs, wonders, and miracles, the Azusa Street revival is the past century's greatest outpouring of the Holy Spirit. Coming to America from a two-year fourteen nation world mission outreach, Ambassadors Gwyneth and Star Williams were in to ignite and spread the flames of the Greater Awakening. They carry the DNA of the Azusa Street Revival throughout the nation and the world. Imparting the gifts of the Holy Spirit with signs, wonders, healings, and miracles.

Outside of celebrating 32 years of international missions and evangelism, Ambassadors Gwyneth and Star ministered in 30 cities and 12 states in 2016. They were carrying revival fire of the Holy Spirit to the Church, Media, Arts & Entertainment, Business, Government, Family, and Education. While in the U.S. they also ordained and commissioned other apostles and appreciated faithful servants in the ministry through certification and commendations.

They take it seriously as they carry the actual and prophetic Power-of-Attorney from the Azusa Street Revival, passed to them by their Dad, Bishop Otis G. Clark who attended the original Azusa Street Mission. He was mentored by the founding members; and faithfully carried the torch (for more than 90 years) of the Azusa Street Revival that was passed to him in the early 1920's.

They continue to carry and fan the flames at events, church service, home meeting, or organizational events and a dynamic anointing of the Holy Spirit for signs, wonders, and miracles.

Azusa Now
Haiti and Colombia July 2013 Mission

While in Colombia and Haiti they ministered to thousands in crusades, churches, and youth outreaches. Ambassador Star took her Set Apart Mentorship Program to the youth - Letting them know: Through Jesus' Holy Spirit, the preached the word of God to the masses, and deliverance of those bound by demonic powers. They had numerous opportunities to share the gospel of Jesus Christ and the love He offers to all mankind! People's lives were eternally changed, many had God encounters and experiences. Many repented and declared to change and live a pure life. They are royalty and are called to be Set Apart unto the Lord.

Missions and evangelism are their passion and they were honored for the opportunity to serve in Port-au-Prince, Jeremie, Haiti and numerous cities in, Colombia.

Over 45 million people in Colombia, it is the 29th largest country in the world and second most populated in South America. With 90% of the religion Roman Catholic, a high unemployment rate, and 50% of the population below the poverty line, Colombia is ripe for the Good News of the Gospel of Jesus Christ. There were many signs and wonders. The people are hungry for the move of God. There has been a great influx of the Baptism of the Holy Spirit and the Azusa outpouring in Colombia. Once Colombia was known as the drug capital of the world. Through much prayer Colombia began to fill the stadiums. Thousands of people were baptized with the fire of God.

Cali, Colombia-Azusa Now

One of the events that transformed the Pentecostal church to another level in Colombia was the death of Julio Ruibals. Ruibals was influenced by Kathrine Kulhman Ministries. He was an evangelist from Bolivia. In 1978 he became a full-time minister in Cali, Colombia. He was martyred in 1995. He received death threats days before he was martyred. It is reported he was killed by professional assassins. Before his death he led an awesome prayer and evangelistic outreach. He trained leaders and many people were giving their lives to God, ex-drug addicts, assassins, prostitutes, people from every walk of life.

After he was murdered authorities believed it was the Cali drug cartel who ordered the hit on his life. What Satan meant for bad God turned it out for the good. Many of the sons and daughters of the ministry continued the legacy. Auditoriums were filled and a greater awakening for Colombia is still prevalent today.

Ambassadors Gwyneth and Star have ministered on two occasions two months in Colombia. They have done 45 outreaches, many testimonies of healings, miracles and the presence of God, is in Colombia. They continue to ignite the fires of Azusa.

They ministered in the Largest Nazarene church in the world of 14,000 members. The pastors of the church, as a prophetic act, repented to Ambassadors Gwyneth and Star on behalf of those who closed their doors to Azusa Street Revival.

Haiti-Azusa Now

Haiti is the poorest country in the Western Hemisphere, most densely populated and least developed country in the world. Ravaged by the 2010 earthquake and much oppression, Haiti needs the Word of God like never before. Humanitarian aid is needed, but also the Word of God preached with demonstration and power. From their recent experience, Haitians are hungry for the truth, the way, and the life.

The problems in these nations are not simply of natural origin, but of spiritual origin. Imagine what a people who have a dream can accomplish. Who are empowered to win. Who know their intrinsic worth, value, and identity. They can walk in the authority of Jesus and the Devil will have to go. They can pull the eternal blessings from the spiritual realm. Imagine a people, created in the image of the Creator waking up to their divine identity and all the endless possibilities. This has been their central message.

Ambassadors Gwyneth & Star have done extensive ministry in Haiti in pastors' meeting. Three days of pastors and leader's meetings. They went to Colombia in Fall 2013 to show compassion and bless the people there, for two weeks in 2013 and six weeks in 2017. They traveled to Haiti July 2013.

God is richly blessing their obedience, as they, go forth and "Go into all the world, preaching the gospel to every creature" Mark 16:15; "Teaching them to observe all things-commanded you" Matthew 28:20.

The detail of the Haiti July 2013 Mission outreach included, "Fruit of Holy Spirit outpouring with our Lord and Savior Jesus Christ. Praise the Lord for a blessed and fruitful mission to Jeremie, Haiti."

Haiti Testimonies

Listed below are detailed highlights of the outreach. Ambassadors Gwyneth and Star ministered every day to youth and pastors. They led a Set Apart youth outreach with over 150 youth and young adults in attendance daily. In addition, they ministered being Set Apart in an orphanage of girls. The girls received an Impartation of worth, identity, heirship and royalty through teaching from the Book of Esther. The girls were crowned with a tiara. They taught and counseled one-on-one a group of young adult women leaders of the crusade staff. They recall the Set-Apart young adults conference in Haiti:

> "The church was full everyone was packed in like sardines. They were eager to hear the Good News about who they are in Christ, God's plan for them sexually and relationally, and His Power to keep them pure."

They taught the Word of God concerning sexuality, fornication, lust, adultery, chastity, and holiness. The Pastor of the host church responded to their eagerness and readiness to learn by saying "They've never heard a teaching like this...they are eager and open to the message." The message was like fresh bread to them, empowering them in wisdom to live a successfully holy single life for Jesus while patiently waiting in faith for the spouse that God has for them.

The last day each person made a commitment to the Lord to surrender their life: body, soul and spirit. People were baptized with the Holy Spirit throughout the outreach.

The Pastors conference released the ministers in their call to five-fold ministry. The team imparted the fire and power of the Holy Spirit for them to go and be witnesses throughout Haiti. They were commissioned to walk in their authority and Kingdom dominion. One pastor testified that he needed this meeting. He was so blessed and encouraged in his call. Identificational repentance was taught referring to the history of Haiti and ties with voodoo. (Daniel 9, 2 Samuel 21)

During the evening meetings the Lord moved mightily through Pearl Ministries, with whom they partnered:

There were hundreds of testimonies throughout the outreach. Each night people lined up to give testimony. Ambassador Gwyneth prayed for a woman who had x-rays of her broken ribs. Her husband beat her. She received Christ and through prayer her ribs were healed.

There were 950 Salvations recorded on paper. Over 1,000 commitments made hundreds of healing miracles testimonies on stage and many more. The crowd reached 12,000, in a town of about 36,000. A man was very ill and wheel chair bound, the next night he came back to testify that Jesus healed him. He was jumping, and leaping, and praising God! Over 4,000 gospel literature booklets were distributed in French.

God is faithful! They thank and praise Him for the opportunity to partner with Him in bringing the Good News to Haiti and keeping the revival fire lit. They prepared for missions to China for the Chopstick Revival; Europe; and America.

God blessed them a 100-fold 1000 times to release the Holy Spirit fire. The gospel was preached. The Lord did mighty work in the midst as He is awakening and reviving His people. They were In Japan and Korea, for several months. God has used Ambassadors Gwyneth and Star in ministry of reconciliation, deliverance, healing, encouragement, youth outreach, and souls for the kingdom. They are doing a particular work in healing and restoring the history and writing a new history for the nations of Japan, Korea, and China.

Azusa Now Anniversary

They prepared for Life Enrichment Ministries 30th Anniversary of taking mission teams to the nations; and Azusa Mission Revival yearly celebration tour through 30 states ministering in churches, schools, to governmental leaders, youth, and pastors. It's time for an awakening in America. Their theme prayer and messages, we are His people. The earth is in pains as in child birth waiting for the sons and daughters of God to arise. "This Is Why We're Here USA outreach" was a huge success. Many people were inspired to fulfill their call.

Brazil Azusa Now

The Azusa mission is to bring revival to ministries, homes, and businesses coast to coast and around the world; and to be faithful to the Kingdom of God! They are doing the Great Commission. Lives are being changed as they follow the leading of the Holy Spirit. In Brazil they ministered in the IDE International Missions Congress with delegates from Africa, Peru, Colombia, Holland, and Chile, Cristo Salva Conferencia de Celulas Open Air Outreach, March for Jesus in Jundiai, Sao Paulo, Teaching at the Foursquare College, Sao Paulo, (Foursquare Church was founded by Aimee Semple McPherson) and Building Godly & Healthy Relationship Seminar at Caieiras Foursquare. Many other outreaches and revival meetings in Curitiba, Belo Horizonte, Campinas, Barueri and more.

They are continuing to run with the torch and mandate that was passed to them from the 1906 Azusa Street Revival, from their Dad, Bishop Otis G. Clark. During 2014 and 2015 for 22 months they ministered in 14 nations, 4 continents, 400 outreaches. They are seeing first hand, the Great Awakening of God in progress!

They are seeing the Book of Acts Church come alive with the empowerment of the Holy Spirit and the witness of Christ Jesus. When they were in Brazil, nearly every sign, wonder and miracle took place: blind eyes opened, ailments gone, Baptism in Holy Spirit and Fire, salvations, healings!

In addition, empowering the next generation through walking in the supernatural has been a great highlight of the outreaches. Many of the youth and young adults baptized in the power and fire of the Holy Spirit. This is priceless, nothing compares in the world to seeing young people set ablaze for God and surrendering their lives completely to the Lord.

"Only one life will soon be past, only what's done for Christ will last." We are living in exciting, yet terrifying times. With wars and rumors of wars we are seeing a shifting in the seasons. The Lord is returning soon, and He's preparing a people for His return. A people without spot or wrinkle. Holiness is being preached, too.

Asia Azusa Now

They continue to share the fire of the Holy Spirit in Asia! The latest updates from the mission field, since the United Kingdom, the Lord has led them to Singapore; Okinawa, Japan; and Johor, Malaysia to share the fire of the Holy Spirit. They are grateful to report that God is still faithful. They survived a Super Typhoon; 7 Magnitude earthquake; and humidity. They spoke peace to the atmosphere and there was a sign and wonder. The super typhon decreased its speed right before coming to the shore line after evacuations of planes and people.

Also, they ministered in the Imparting Pentecostal Fire for Revival conference in 2014 in Singapore with 95-year-old evangelist Dr. Verna Linzey, who went home to be with the Lord in 2017. They went to Okinawa, Japan to a body of believers and pastors who wanted the Azusa fires released and an impartation of reconciliation. In addition, they imparted at a weekend youth retreat; ministered in the Geylang community of Singapore, a red-light district where sex trafficking is prevalent; and in Malaysia to new believers who've renounced idol and ancestry worship.

The impartation of the Azusa ministry continues. The Lord, working through them has been making divine kingdom connections worldwide. They are linking with key end time people who come together for the work of the Kingdom. Now is the time for the bench-warmers to get in the game. No spectators here.

Prophesy fulfilled: While in Brazil in April, 2014. Dr. Gwyneth received a Prophetic word about going to Japan where she'd meet a man with white hair who's been interceding for The Awakening and "is waiting for you to come help them." Like the Macedonia call in Acts 16:9. The Lord supernaturally made a way for us to go to Japan during the historical Japan Homecoming event. A gathering of Asians from Japan, China, and many other nations. The Lord moved mightily. During the meeting we met the man with white hair. We were invited to the follow up meeting with key pastors in Okinawa and was able to share our heart and mission to see The Awakening. They excitedly looked forward to returning to Japan and Southeast Asia in November 2015 to work with Apostle Paul while strengthening and planting churches.

In 2015, they returned and many signs, wonders and miracles were manifest, They spent 5 months in Asia releasing the fire of God and rekindling the Azusa Revival.

> "The wind blows wherever it pleases. You hear its sound, but you cannot tell where it comes from or where it is going. So, it is with everyone born of the Spirit." John 3:8

In Brazil, they carried the fire and power of the Holy Spirit to the nations. They were there for 5 months. They are delighted to share these testimonies and updates from the mission field. God has been doing amazing miracles, signs, wonders, and healings in their midst.

On April 20 2014, Resurrection Sunday, this young man's life (pictured) changed forever. He had been shot in the leg in his femur bone. The doctor's prognosis wasn't good, and his only hope was for God to perform a miracle.

When they first met him, he was barely standing in the prayer line on crutches and with his friends on either side assisting him. He was waiting for us to lay hands on him and pray the prayer of faith for healing. His faith was there to be healed. You could sense the expectation and desire to be touched by God.

Once the prayer was made the Power of God shot through his body, the crutches went away and he ran around the church, by himself with no assistance. Since then he hasn't used crutches and walks normally. When they returned to the church three months later, they received a pleasant surprise, when the pastor announced that he was there. To testify and show God's power, he came out of his seat and did a running double flip down the aisle of the church and landed on his feet! God is so good. He is Healer, Savior, and Deliver! This is one example of what God is doing in our midst! Healed of a gunshot wound in the femur bone. There is no God like our God who acts for the one who  waits for him, Isaiah 64:4. We are the church Holy Spirit and Azusa Now, like the book of Acts.

> "Faith does not operate in the realm of the possible. There is no glory for God in that which is humanly possible. Faith begins where man's power ends." George Mueller

Continuing the Legacy 2017-2018

Ambassadors Star and Gwyneth visited Eleven countries with the Azusa message of signs and wonders and reconciliation during this, 18 months, 78 weeks, 300 meetings and revivals in Colombia, Argentina, Uruguay, South Africa, Mozambique, Lesotho, Uganda, Kenya, Tanzania, Egypt, and Israel.

Tens of thousands of souls touched for the Kingdom of God, they have ministered in open air meetings, tent revivals, jails, rehabilitation detention center, youth, children and women's ministry, leadership meetings, schools, governments, villages, churches, homes, and on television and radio. They have been to eleven countries on 3 continents and have not returned to the United States in One Year and eight months. Even as they are writing this update in July of 2018, they do not plan to return to the United States until 2020. They often say the world is their neighborhood.

Highlighted Testimonies

They have experienced the Lord accomplishing mighty wonders, salvations, and healings. A girl bound by loneliness and depression was set free and set on fire with the power of the Holy Spirit. Many of the alter calls people have been baptized with the Holy Spirit and fire of God. Some people while sitting in their seats, too.

A pastor's son named Elijah had walked away from God to the world where he experienced hurt, pain and bad things. When he came back to God and the church he found the joy and the peace he was looking for. He was baptized dramatically in the fire of God. Slain in the spirit on the floor weeping and receiving from God.

A pastor's wife was electrified with the Holy Spirit's fire. Something she had not experienced in over 30 years! Many people have been renewed in the meetings and had not experienced God like that in years or for the first time.

Congregations fell under the glory cloud and could not move. The presence of God was so intense they sit in holy hushes under the glory cloud of the Lord as they enter into the Holies of Holies. Many people experienced the Shekinah Glory of God in the meetings.

Many youth set apart, sanctified, and set on fire with the Holy Spirit. These are a few of the many miraculous and supernatural encounters that are taking place on a daily basis!

Journal excerpt:

In Lesotho, Africa: "Church has no indoor plumbing (we use outdoor toilets) no heat or air conditioning. They are faithful servants. We ministered in the Pastor's and Leadership Meeting, Youth and General meeting. It was a Holy Spirit Encounter at Logos Rhema. The Messages: Prayer Births Transformation, Hindrances to Prayer, Here I am Send me. The Pastors signed the unity prayer quilt. It was a 4 Hour Training Session. We Love our job!!!! Saturday Night Youth Service The youth took an extension cord down the road to have lights for the service, so dedicated. Star's Message: The Power of One, being World Changers and receiving the Holy Spirit's empowerment. Ministered to the Minister of

Finance Officials in Lesotho. Message: They were Appointed for Such a Time as This as they administrate the finances for their Country Lesotho. We prayed they would know God as Jehovah El Shaddai, and Jehovah Jireh."

Two Day Women's Meeting Africa and other meetings, as a prophetic act each women, young girls and adults were crowned. Message: Rise up Esthers, Deborahs and Women of God. It was a powerful move of the Holy Spirit during the service. Thank you Lord for souls for the kingdom.

Prophetic Mapping

Prayer mapping and prophetic acts is a part of the ministries they activate. They have done them in the above mentioned nations. These proclamations and acts in the Pacific, Atlantic, Indian Oceans, Arabian Peninsula, the Red China Sea, Lake Victoria, the Nile River Egypt and Uganda. They have prayed for peace at the junction of the three rivers that flow into North and South Korea. Reconciliation, revival, awakening and other proclamations. The Rift, Nyaharuru Falls, renamed Holy Spirit Flow.

Unity Prayer Quilt

The Unity Prayer Quilt representing the Body of Christ has over 550 leaders, bishops, and pastors from many nations: Asia, Europe, Africa and North & South Americas and the Middle East. It's over 100 feet long and takes 10 tall men to hold up to display.

Ambassador Gwyneth had a dream while in Japan, in 2015. The Lord spoke to her after showing her a white washed wall and His hand sewing together prayer clothes next to the wall. He spoke to her to tell the leaders, He wants them to come together and not be like the Pharisees. In April 2015 they started having the leaders pray for unity and sign the prayer clothes.

White washed is a literal Greek translation. It is where a dirty wall has been made to appear clean. In this case they are referred to as hypocrites one who looks clean. When it refers to people it is a person who seems to look good or doing right but is not.

God spoke to her through the dream; He was saying the church leaders needed to come together in unity. They appear to love one another, but privately they were destroying their brothers and sisters with harsh words, gossip, competition, jealousy, and black listing.

He spoke to her to take this quilt to the uttermost parts of the earth and tell His leaders, they are better together. When each leader signs this quilt they are making a statement to remain in unity, fast their words and no competitive jealousy. To date the quilt has gone to South Korea, Taiwan, France, Eiffel tower, England, Wales, Spain, United States, Colombia, Argentina, Uruguay, South Africa, Mozambique, Lesotho, Uganda, Kenya, Tanzania, Egypt, and Israel. The theme of the prayer quilt is "We are Better Together."

Azusa Lamp

In addition, the Azusa Lamp and Prayer Quilt have been utilized together in Asia. Apostles, Prophets, Evangelist, Pastors and Teachers have signed and prayed for unity in The Body of Christ as mentioned above. The lamp has been utilized to bring unity, too. The prophetic acts have been, Love One Another. The prophetic acts with the lamp have been for decrees and proclamations, but for unity among churches, leaders, and nations.  The oil was utilized before Azusa at a revival put on by the Tuthill family in Houston, Texas. Seymour was there as Parham read the Bible with the oil in the lamp. Ambassadors Gwyneth and Star are blessed, honored and privileged to be carriers of the oil. Roberta Tuthill currently has one of the three lamps used at the revival in Houston.

The Azusa Oil Lamp has been to these places of ministry Japan, Brazil, Singapore, Malaysia, Korea, Taiwan, China, Hong Kong, England, Wales, Spain, France, America, Colombia, Uruguay, Argentina, South Africa, Mozambique, Lesotho, Uganda, Tanzania, Kenya, Egypt, Dubai, and Israel. Their goal is to keep the Azusa fire of the Holy Spirit ignited and souls for the kingdom of God.

The Azusa Lantern is a prophetic symbol of the Holy Spirit's Fire, power & presence. Part of the mandate is to ignite and re-dig wells of the Azusa Street Revival. The lantern has oil from a lantern used by Charles Parham sent to Ambassadors Gwyneth and Star by Roberta Tuthill. It was used when he read the Bible as Brother William J. Seymour looked on. The lantern was lit at Bishop Otis Clark's memorial service. Ambassadors Gwyneth & Star carried it out of the service as a prophetic act that they would carry the Holy Spirit and Fire to the nations of the earth! And that is exactly what they are doing with the gracious help of the Lord.

In addition, the Azusa Street Lamp has been, so far, to several cities in the United States, to continue the legacy and remind the saints of the Hope. It's been lit hundreds of times! As they minister and call on the Holy Spirit's help, they are seeing the power and presence of God show up in marvelous ways. Revival is touching the nations of the earth. There is a hunger for the Lord. They are believing and praying for the Third Wave of Refreshing. They have seen pockets of revival.

As you celebrate the Azusa Street revival be reminded to fan the flame of the Holy Spirit within you. The church must welcome back the presence and power of the Holy Spirit. Let Him not be extinct within the Body of Christ. Now is the time of Awakening! Now is the time to unleash the Holy Spirit with signs, wonders and miracles! Where the Spirit of the Lord is, there is Freedom (2 Corinthians 3:17).

Supernatural Provision

During most of the holidays they minister in outreaches and mission endeavors reaching many souls for Christ. God is good and always faithful when they give themselves to the kingdom! They are thankful for the supernatural, provision, prayers and support! With excitement and great joy in all the Lord has done. He has been their Ebenezer and they have come this far by His grace and faith to continue. They trust God for all finances and do not take a salary. They continue daily in prayer. God is their Jehovah Jireh, Jehovah El Shaddai. They stand on the scripture and take it literal that everything they need God provides. Matthew 6:33, "Seek first His kingdom, His power, and His righteousness and everything you need will be added unto you." This is the scripture they stand on to be a blessing to the nations of the world.

Testimonies of God's provision and providence are a daily occurrence. As they daily walk by faith they see the Lord stepping in to provide food, housing and remarkable opportunities. They are daily amazed at His goodness toward them!

School Outreaches

During one of the school outreaches all the children asked Jesus to be their Savior and Lord! What a special day for them reaching the next generation it was an open heaven. They were both crying when they left the stage. Awesome and moving experience!

Another school outreach in Africa was a High School, 90% of the gangs in South Africa come from that school. Some of the students are from Soweto, and Randburg. The Holy Spirit's empowerment was manifest.

In addition, Westbury school, Fourteen hundred Students heard the Gospel and 1,200 raised their hand and accepted Jesus by saying the sinner's prayer. The children sit on the ground for full assembly because they have classrooms only and no auditorium. Ambassador Star's message: "Your Body is the Temple of the Holy Spirit." She shares her testimony of remaining a virgin, practicing holiness, by the Holy Spirit's empowerment.

Also, a School Outreach in Africa was in Dowling, Africa. Nine hundred students and 750 in this assembly asked Jesus in their hearts. Message: "Agents of Change: Holiness, Purity and Purpose."

Pentecost and Passover

Passover and Pentecost are two of the three major biblical pilgrimage festivals and represents a time of harvest. There is a spiritual significance to the season of the counting of Omer that leads to Pentecost, held 50 days after resurrection Sunday and begins at Passover. This represents the 40-day period that Jesus appeared to His disciples before He ascended into heaven.

In the Old Covenant the Passover was the time of the deliverance of the Israelites from slavery and bondage in Egypt. God had a plan to deliver them, He gave His people instruction on how He would deliver them, it involved the sacrifice of a lamb, spreading the blood over the doorpost of their house, and preparing the lamb to eat with unleavened bread; and ultimately fleeing from Egypt. With the spoils and unbaked bread in tow, they fled Egypt quickly in the middle of the night. His purpose for delivering Israel was their freedom to worship Him (Exodus 7:16).

Now it came to pass, when Jesus had finished all these sayings, that He said to His disciples, You know that after two days is the Passover, and the Son of Man will be delivered up to be crucified" Matthew 26:1. Jesus, our Passover lamb once and for all became the only sacrifice that would ever be needed for freedom.

He instructed them to wait for the promised Holy Spirit, who would comfort them and lead and guide them into all truth (John 14:26; 16:13). Then as 120 disciples were in the upper room in one accord, the promised Holy Spirit manifested upon each of them.

> "And being assembled together with them, He commanded them not to depart from Jerusalem, but to wait for the Promise of the Father, "which," He said, "you have heard from Me; But you shall receive power when

> the Holy Spirit has come upon you; and you shall be witnesses to Me in Jerusalem, and in all Judea and Samaria, and to the end of the earth." Acts 1:4,8

> "When the Day of Pentecost had fully come, they were all with one accord in one place. And suddenly there came a sound from heaven, as of a rushing mighty wind, and it filled the whole house where they were sitting. Then there appeared to them divided tongues, as of fire, and one sat upon each of them. And they were all filled with the Holy Spirit and began to speak with other tongues, as the Spirit gave them utterance" Acts 2:1-4.

Pentecost, also known as Shavuot in the New Covenant; and the celebration of God giving Moses the Ten Commandments on Mount Sinai (Exodus 19) in the Old Covenant is approaching and each year the church should anticipate what God is doing in this season as He pours out His spirit afresh on His people.

God promised that when the Holy Spirit came: He would write His law on the hearts of His people, and no longer on tablets of stone:

"For this is the covenant that I will make with the house of Israel after those days, says the Lord: I will put My laws in their mind and write them on their hearts; and I will be their God, and they shall be My people. None of them shall teach his neighbor, and none his brother, saying, 'Know the Lord,' for all shall know Me, from the least of them to the greatest of them. For I will be merciful to their unrighteousness, and their sins and their lawless deeds I will remember no more" Hebrews 8:11.

10

Signs, Wonders & The Anointing

Signs & Wonders

"The church today is seeking for the truth and value of God. When you come to God with a soft heart, not a stony heart wanting what He wants. God wants His children to come to the saving grace, trusting in His power to heal, perform signs and wonders in our lives, in the name of Jesus."

The church is the bride of Christ desiring and crying out for the things of God knowing He will answer. Ambassador Gwyneth's personal testimony: when she was a teenager she cried out with everything within her for God to show himself. She cried out, "God if you are God show me Your power." She was picked up in a whirl wind and moved 80 feet. God is real, and He is powerful. This experience helped her put her eyes more on Him and her heart's desire to seek Him more.

Many signs and wonders are done among the people as they minister to the nations. In the New Testament, the apostles laid hands on the people. Believers were added to the church. People are looking for signs and wonders. In the book of Acts and during Azusa people and believers were added to the church. The Lord multiplied the multitudes both men and women, so that they even carried out the sick into the streets and laid them on beds and pallets. As Peter came by at least his shadow might fall on some of them. The people also gathered from the towns around Jerusalem, bringing the sick and those afflicted with unclean spirits, and they were all healed, Acts 5:15,16.

Acts 4:29–30, During this time there was a lot of opposition so that the Christians cried out like the church needs to today: "Lord, look upon their threats, and grant to your servants to speak your word with all boldness, while you stretch out Your hand to heal, and signs and wonders are performed through the name of Your holy servant Jesus." The Azusa Now needs a louder cry of boldness in witness. Let the church cry even louder for God's hand to be stretched forth in healing. Let them believe and cry for God to perform more signs and wonders. During Azusa and now Ambassador Gwyneth and Star are not just wanting signs and wonders they cry out in the meetings for God to reveal His glory and pray for miracles to come. They are seeing them, too.

During New Testament times and Azusa, there were first hand experiences. Clark, Cotton, and Seymour were able to have eye witness experiences of the Signs and Wonders.

> *"The Azusa now is the Joshua generation believing and crying out for more power, and more evidence of the truth. Holy Spirit in the Now is what the church needs."*

This is the generation of witnesses of the Azusa Outpouring whose word was least in need of supernatural authentication of all the generations following. This was the generation whose preaching, teaching, miracles were done by the Holy Spirit. The book of Acts and at Azusa many souls came to Christ.

The New Testament times many witnessed the miracles even the resurrection, but still wanted more. God is calling His people to a higher place of praise and seeking His power. He wanted the same things for the children of Israel. The preaching and demonstration of Paul, Peter and the disciples is for the body of Christ today to stretch out their hands and heal the sick; the cry of the church for God's healing power and for His signs and wonders is vital.

When Ambassadors Gwyneth and Star do their outreaches, they are looking for souls for the kingdom and to see the expression of God's power. The church wants and is praying for a Greater Awakening and the gifts of the Spirit manifest in the church. The demonstration of signs and wonders is seen, people in Jerusalem, unbelievers in awe of the apostles and the church. In Acts, Ananias and Sapphira had died some people were God fearing and seekers, healings and miracles were being done.

Acts 5:12: "Many signs and wonders were done among the people by the hands of the apostles. And they were all together in Solomon's Portico." Vs.13 "None of the rest dared join them, but the people held them in high honor." But that's not all. Amid all this fear and amazement and wonder, many were coming to faith in Jesus. Vs. 14 "And more than ever believers were added to the Lord, multitudes both of men and women."

During Azusa and now there is evidence in the meetings where miracles are the result of leading people to salvation. They see the Holy Spirit moving and want more of God. The Spirit draws them. Therefore, many conversions are seen in the book of Acts. The miracle of Pentecost led to 3,000 converts and the miracle of the lame man in Acts 3:6 lead to 2,000 converts. Many people heard the word and believed; and it grew to 5000, Acts 4:4.

Also, Peter heals Aeneas in Acts 9:32-35; "And all the residents of Lydda and Sharon saw him, and they turned to the Lord." In addition, Peter raises Tabitha from the dead, and Luke says, "It became known throughout all Joppa, and many believed in the Lord."

Ambassador Gwyneth and Star when they minister around the world emphasize the working of miracles, signs and wonders, they can help bring people to Christ. This is what is stated in Luke. He wants Christians to stretch forth their hands to heal and do signs and wonders. It would help bring people to Christ. Signs and wonders are a witness to the Word of God. When they minister people are amazed at His presence and desire more. They minister the Word of God, and signs and wonders follow. Many testimonies draw new people to the meetings to hear the Word and experience God. The signs and wonders complement the services they have and help some to salvation.

The Anointing

> *"You have been given the mantle to carry on the power of the Holy Spirit for the next 60 years, 40 years, or 30 years on this earth, how will you use your time?" Luke 4:18 "The Spirit of the Lord is upon Me, because He has anointed Me to preach the gospel to the poor." As Christ's disciples He has given you that same anointing and same calling to walk in the power and the anointing of God. He's saying the same power that raised Jesus from the dead resides within you. The same power and anointing that is upon Jesus is upon you. You are to minister to the poor not to be poor. The Holy Spirit is reaching out to you so that you can go to another level and see the greater spiritual awakening you are waiting for. He has sent me to proclaim freedom for the prisoners. We are called to be good news carriers. You are called as a good news carrier.*

Many people in the church have been missing their part because they are just spectators. God is not looking for spectators that are sitting in the pews watching but He is looking for proclaimers of the gospel of Jesus. To make the proclamation in their own lives, families, church, community, towns, villages, and to the utter most parts of the earth. So that the oppressed might be set free, not that the church is oppressed needing to be set free. He's called the body of Christ to see and have the anointing in their lives. To proclaim freedom for the prisoner and recovery of sight to the blind, and to set the oppressed free. That is the mandate that has been given to all the body of Christ not only a select few. That is the mandate that was given to Christ. The Lord wants to take the body of Christ higher. He wants to take them to another level. He wants all His people to live under an open heaven. So that the blessings of the Lord will make rich and add no sorrow, Proverbs 10:22.

What is the Anointing?

The word Anointed in the Greek is Chiro which means authority. Chiro means anointed - the authority and ability to perform God's will. With that authority there is an ability. God is saying, if the body of Christ is going to walk in the anointing they must rise into a greater authority.

> *He is calling us to go into greater levels of authority. You hold as a child of God a higher authority than any person upon the earth because you are a son or daughter of God. Anointing means to walk in the authority and to have the ability. Are you able? Are you able to take territory? Are you able to take nations? Are you able to defeat the demons in your own life that are trying to harass you? Under the anointing of God, you have the authority and you have the ability. That is the anointing. It's not about you. The anointing is about the kingdom of God. He empowers you to walk in the authority and have the ability to walk in the blessings and the manifestation to do kingdom business. The Lord is saying it's time to wake up, and to walk in the manifestation of the blessing. Are you performing the will of God to the highest level of the ability and purpose*

God called you here to earth? You've made it to earth for these 120 years that you've been promised. What will you do with those years? Will you live to the fullest level and perform God's will? Do you want to go to another level? He wants to enlarge your borders and expand your tent pegs.

Supernatural Strength

Charles Spurgeon said, a church without the spirit, a church without the anointing, a church that has come to the level of religiosity is a curse rather than a blessing. As the body of Christ, if you have not the spirit and anointing of God remember that you stand in someone else's way because you have become fruitless, without anointing. You're standing where a fruitful tree might grow.

The anointing is the authority and ability to perform God's will with the supernatural strength. When the church is anointed, they are endowed with supernatural power. In the Bible, those whom God anointed were able to do the will of God. David was anointed to slay Goliath. When everyone else was all dressed up, like the church today and not participating in the will of God, David accomplished the will of God with supernatural strength. Christianity is not a spectator's sport. God has called everyone to be a part of His will and His kingdom manifesting.

The Lord wants the church to be anointed to use His supernatural strength and ability to perform His will. The Lord wants everyone not just to spectate, not just to watch but to be involved in what He's doing - as apostles, prophets, pastors, teachers, and evangelists with signs, wonders and miracles following. The world will go to the palm readers, the psychics, and the voodoo priests while believers have the prophetic word and word of knowledge that needs to be released under the supernatural power with the ability to see someone's life changed. The Lord wants to bring a greater anointing back to the church. It's time for the church to arise, take territory, take over for the Kingdom and know who she is in Christ. That is why believers are on earth - to populate heaven and de-populate hell.

> *"You are on the earth to let others know that Jesus died, He was buried, He rose on the third day and He took the keys of death, hell and the grave that they may live (Eph. 4:9; Rev. 1:18). He said I will send you the Holy Spirit, you shall be baptized in the Holy Spirit and with the fire of God. That is the supernatural power and the anointing God wants His church to walk in."*

God is calling the church at the end of time that they would walk in a greater authority and a greater anointing because the world is saying that there is no fruit and no love in the church. Some youth are saying there's more power in the world and they'd rather serve Satan. The devil has concerts with people singing and levitating themselves. They see the counterfeit. When the anointing and the power is within the church, people will say "What must I do to be saved? How can I get that anointing, how can I get the fire of God, how can I get this thirst quenched?" The power lies within the believer, not the pastor solely. If the church doesn't use the power the next generation will go to the concerts and they'll see the tables levitate by the satanic power of a false god; but they're waiting to see the supernatural power, ability and authority within the church.

Manifestations of the Blessing

Two things Christians ask for prayer mostly. First, they believe they have a curse. How can the church be anointed of God full of the power of the Holy Spirit, with the ability, power and strength of God and have a curse on their life? That is the number one prayer request at altar calls all over the world. God wants to stir the Holy Spirit to take the church higher because the church has become powerless. He wants to stir the fire of the Holy Spirit. So that a bible believing Christian will know that no altar with a name written on by Satan can have more power than the blood of Jesus and the anointing of God. Many in the church believe in old traditions and superstitions. They believe they are under a curse. One cannot be cursed unless they open the doors and the windows to give the demons, devils and Satan permission. When believers are anointed of God, the anointing will break the yoke of Satan off their life. How can Christians be oppressed? How can the anointed of God be depressed when they have the mind of Christ? The Lord is going to stir the church to go to another level that they may know and have supernatural ability, and supernatural strength to do great exploits. The second most asked prayer request is to receive courage.

> *If you are anointed of God, the devil cannot grip you. If you're anointed of God, the enemy cannot come and take territory. If the church has the courage, then all doubt must leave because you have the faith to move mountains. The Lord wants His church to live under an open heaven and to walk in the blessings. Where the angels are chasing you down to give you the blessing of the manifestation because you are expecting. You're walking under the anointing of God. Many blessings that the enemy has made the church miss is because they've been fruitless. It's time for the church to arise and to go to a higher dimension to receive the harvest of the blessings. The church has missed their own blessings because of complaining and unbelief.*

God is a God of recompense, He is Jehovah Gemolah. When Peter came to the door and knocked. Rhoda answered the door, but she was in unbelief. Peter was in jail and the angel of the Lord came to assist him. Not only was Peter in jail but he was chained on both sides with two guards. The church was praying in the house that is the formality of the church, they're praying but the angel came, and the chains broke under the anointing of God. The angel was knocking at the door bringing the blessing, that's why believers must stay under the anointing and expectation (Acts 12).

> *The chains in your life that is keeping you from the supernatural are broken off your life. The angel said get up quickly and get dressed. Peter thought it was a dream. He gets up, the angel goes past the other guard and opens the door. God will open doors for you by an angelic host of heaven. Follow the instructions like Peter followed the angel out of prison. Under the anointing blessings are coming to you. You may have missed blessings because the spirit of determent has tried to stop you. A spirit has tried to deter you, but God is saying that under the anointing of God you will have the ability and you will be able to receive those blessings.*

When the angel supernaturally opened the door, he went to the house and Rhoda did not open the door because she did not expect her prayers to be answered. Even the people in the prayer meeting did not believe. When Rhoda said Peter is knocking at the door, they said she was out of her mind (Acts 12:13-17). It is time for the church to walk under the anointing, go to another level, and receive the supernatural manifestations from God.

> *The doors will open so that you will have a greater supernatural anointing. Why is it that everyone around the world looks at the superheroes? Jesus and the anointing of God is the greatest superhero that we could ever need. The Holy Spirit and power of God is the greatest*

power we can have. Tell the Holy Spirit right now that you need Him. Tell Him that you need His anointing, you need the Shekinah and you need the glory in your life. The world wants to see the Spirit's fire, flame and the blaze within the church.

The Cost of the Anointing

How does one lose the anointing? Disobedience is the number one thing that causes the children of God to miss the blessing and lose the anointing upon their lives. In the prophetic or whatever gift God has given, He wants believers to be obedient stewards. A price that must be paid to walk in the anointing. When someone is not obedient to follow the things that God has said to do or pay the price, they lose the promise of God. With the anointing there is a price that must be paid. Years ago, Ambassador Gwyneth had a dream: She states as follows,

"Everywhere I could see from the north, south, east and west were multitudes and multitudes of little baby chickens. As the Overseer of these little baby chickens walked me down the road I could see at the end of the road thick kernels of maize. The chicks were trying to pick at the maize, but their beaks were the size of the corn. I looked down to pick up one and then looked at the Shepherd whom I knew was Lord. I asked the cost for the baby chick because I wanted to take one to my daughter. He told me they are $500 each. Would you pay $500 for a little baby chick? I awoke and went to Seminary that morning and a great prophet of modern-day walked into the café where I was and he said someone here had a dream last night and God sent me to interpret it. I shared the dream with him and he interpreted. He said all the little baby chicks represented souls and the Body of Christ. The Shepherd and Overseer was the Lord. A baby chicken cannot eat maize that big. He said, "God has called you to the Body of Christ to help them grow up to be able to eat the large

> *kernels of maize, so you could lead them across to the other side." He said the reason they were $500 is because the price that you must pay for the anointing and for ministry is great."*

Many people will not pay the price; therefore, they miss the blessing and they miss walking in the anointing. With the anointing there is a price that must be paid. In dire times like these it requires an anointing that can break the yokes of bondage off people who are so much in despair.

The Quenching Agents

The church is at a crossroads. Will there be judgment, or will there be an awakening? Much of the church does not believe in judgment or that hell exists. Revival depends upon the Body of Christ arising and walking in the divine purpose that God has for the church. If the church does not arise the anointing will be extinguished and extinct within the Body of Christ. Some Pentecostal churches have almost become like a lukewarm church. Going through routine and rituals. They must return to the anointing because it's not about numbers. When the anointing is extinguished it is because flesh arises and quenches the Spirit of the anointing. When the flesh gets involved it's the quenching agent and reason the anointing is broken.

At Azusa when people came into the meeting Seymour spent most of the time sitting behind the pulpit. When they came in he was praying and crying out to God for revival and awakening. He knew it was not about him and it was not about the flesh, but it was about the Holy Spirit and what the Holy Spirit wanted to do in the lives of the people. After the great revival and anointing at Azusa Street the churches unfortunately returned to their formality of dressing; the choirs singing;

and religious rituals. Lacking the power of the Holy Spirit. The flesh came in and quenched the anointing of the Holy Spirit.

Humility before the Lord is a requirement for the anointing to be in one's life. What happened to Saul? The Lord said, "When you were little in your own eyes were you not head of the tribes of Israel?" However, he was sent on a mission and did not obey the instruction of the Lord (1 Samuel 15:17-19). Much competitive jealousy is within the church because some want to be the ones that are the head. They want to be the ones who get the credit.

Like oxen plow with the yoke upon their shoulders. Losing humility puts you back under the yoke of bondage. For example, Saul when he was small in his own eyes, God used him. Partial obedience is still disobedience. Saul was hindered because he did not do what God told him to do. He thought he was doing what was right because he saved the perfect animals to sacrifice to God. However, God specifically told him to kill everything and destroy everyone. Under the anointing, God requires strict obedience. In that obedience one must pray to have 20/20 vision in the spirit realm. Pray that ears are open to hear what the Spirit of the Lord is saying. Many generational curses influence Christians because they cannot see. They miss the blessing.

Even Saul he killed the Gibeonites, but hundreds of years before that Joshua made a covenant. A covenant and someone else's disobedience can cause a drought where there is no anointing so that the blessing is missed. What happened, David the man after God's heart inquired of God. He asked God, "Why this drought. Why am I not receiving the freshness, the oil, and the fruit of the land?" David was not walking in the blessings of God because of someone else's partial obedience. To have identification of what is going on in the spirit realm because the anointing will break the yoke. When David cried out after going through three years of drought he went through identificational repentance. He identified the disobedience. He went to the Gibeonites and there was a sacrifice for him to receive the blessing so that he may flourish in the land (2 Samuel 21).

> *It's important for you to ask the Lord to remove the scales from your eyes so that you can see in the spiritual realm. May God show you things that are generational that you need to deal with in your life that are holding you back. Partial obedience is not obedience.*

God said to Saul, "Because you have rejected the word of the Lord I will reject you as king." This was not a one-time occurrence. Some may think that God does not see what they are doing in secret but He sees all that's why believers need the anointing of God to live daily under repentance - to receive the full anointing. Bishop Clark, Ambassadors Gwyneth and Star would often perform identificational repentance in cities, and families so that they would get breakthroughs. The enemy will try to keep the church down, he will try to deter so they cannot walk in the blessing.

When Ambassadors Gwyneth and Star were in Haiti they had over 90 pastors that they ministered to in the day sessions of the crusade. It took all 90 of the pastors to come together unified to plan, prepare and execute a crusade of 18,000 people in a town of only 34,000 people. When 90 pastors are unified for one mission they can take a city. However, the anointing is quenched, and the church fails when "It's about me," "I'm the head of this and I'm going to be the one who gets the credit."

When they were in Asia a pastor told them about an incident during a crusade with a great American evangelist. The pastors gathered for a large meeting, but he said there was so much infighting among the pastors that when one of the pastors stood up to walk across the room another pastor kicked him right in the middle of his back and ever since then he's had back trouble. It is that type of spirit that quenches the anointing and citywide revival. It's that reason why pastors cannot come together to take nations for the kingdom of God.

While they were in Uganda they were part of three crusades and each crusade had about 10,000 to 12,000 people each night. The people came together. The police officers, the mayors, the governors, everyone was there, and everyone was apart. The anointing of God requires the unity. When the church is anointed, and unified cities can be impacted for Christ. The enemy wants to divide and conquer the church so that no anointing exists, and no citywide revival takes place. During the last crusade in Uganda hundreds of prostitutes came and were delivered. As deliverance was happening their bodies were contorting like snakes on the floor. This deliverance came as result of the church coming together with the anointing of God that brought unity, anointing and deliverance for the people of that city. The yokes were broken off their lives because of the anointing.

Isaiah 10:27, "In that day his burden will be lifted from their shoulders, and his yoke from your neck, and the yoke will be destroyed because of the anointing oil." He's talking about the yoke of the enemy being removed from Israel's neck and shoulders. There are two yolks. First, the yoke the enemy puts upon the Body of Christ and the people in the world. Israel went through much bondage, but the Lord said the burden shall be lifted from their shoulders and the yoke of the enemy broken from their neck. The breaking of the yoke as when Israel was in bondage in Egypt. However, they wanted to go back to the way of living and bondage in Egypt (Numbers 14:4). They wanted to stay under the heavy yoke that pushed them down on their neck. That's what the enemy is trying to do to the church. However, the Lord does not want His people in spiritual bondage because the anointing is what breaks the yoke of bondage off one's life.

Remaining in the Spirit

You do not have to fret or worry because you are in the hands of the Lord. We must hear what He is saying in this season because God's yoke is easy and light. (Matthew 11:28-30). We put that scripture on Bishop Clark's memorial stone. Many people in the church believe the devil is after them every day and he's whipping them. They say he's after me, after my child, he's after my son. The bondage of the Babylonian system will put a yoke around your neck, to choke you and try to kill you; but Jesus says My yoke is easy.

They were in Africa and the plane's engine failed. Ambassador Gwyneth told Bishop Clark after they made the announcement over the intercom that the engine failed. Bishop Clark was sitting next to her and she said, "Dad you should pray because the engine has failed in the plane." She knew it was not her time to leave earth because God has many souls for her to reach. They prayed for the pilot and the peace of God came into the atmosphere after they prayed for him. They had a hot landing; the tire blew out but thank the Lord they were safe. After they landed she said, "That was better than bungee jumping or zip lining."

God's yoke is easy, and His burdens are lights no matter what comes. Believers do not have to go back to the Babylonian system of bondage. They do not have to go back to Egypt. The Lord will take His people, under the anointing, into their promised land. The word of God says, Our Father who art in heaven, hallowed be thy name, thy kingdom come, thy will be done on earth as it is in heaven (Matthew 6:9,10). The Lord says, come to Me all who labor in the flesh. The flesh is what quenches the anointing. The reason why many Christians are not having heaven on earth is because they are taking the burden of Satan upon their shoulders.

> *If you hold on you can have heaven on earth. The Bible says His yoke is easy and His burdens are light. The yoke is broken off your neck when you walk in the anointing. It is the anointing that breaks the yoke of Satan. We're supposed to be walking on earth as we walk in heaven. We are supposed to have heaven on earth. The flesh quenches your blessings, but you can have heaven on earth. The Lord says take His yoke it is easy, His burdens they are light. You take the enemy's yoke if you complain and think that sickness is your friend, diseases are your friends, and that you're under your nation's economy. You're not under the Babylonian system and economy. You're under the kingdom's economy where God's yoke is easy, and His burdens are light!*

Oiled Up

Pastors and leaders must grow up and stop allowing the enemy to push them around. The church must understand the anointing is what breaks the yoke of bondage. Walking in the anointing brings the manifestation of heaven on earth. The Lord says, take His yoke and learn of Him because His yoke is easy.

> *When you are anointed with the oil of God the devil cannot grip you. When you are oiled up with anointing he will not be able to hold on to you. If you are being defeated, then add the oil of anointing to your life. If you are being jerked around when you're anointed it's easy to slip out of his grasp. Are you walking with Jesus? You're not under the Babylonian system but you're under the system of God and the kingdom of God. He says you shall have more than enough. The devil cannot put his hands on you because you are oiled up. That's the anointing of God. It's easy, His burdens are light, but many have accepted the spirit of the fear to take the burdens of Satan.*

Jehovah El Shaddai

Pray that His kingdom comes, and His will is done on earth as it is in heaven. Believers are on earth just like Jesus is in heaven. That is an anointed life and a peaceful life. That is a life of tranquility and that is walking under an open heaven. A life that knows Jehovah Gemolah, and Jehovah Sabaoth. The Lord fights battles under the anointing and for His anointed people. Why would the church want to go back to spiritual bondage when they've been delivered? The anointing of God breaks the yoke of bondage. The yoke that many have carried has deterred them from the blessings of God.

> *The Lord says I am Jehovah El Shaddai you shall have more than enough for distribution. You shall have more than enough. You're not a beggar and you're not in poverty. You are a giver under the anointing of God. You are anointed. The enemy cannot grip your finances, your mind, or your peace. The Lord says because the burdens are light, and His yoke is easy. He is your peace and your Shalom. Nothing missing in your life and nothing broken in your life. Everything you need He provides.*

> *The Holy Spirit is in the now. The decree is that you shall have more than enough and that your barns will be full. You shall walk in more than enough. Jehovah El Shaddai will be your God and every poverty spirit is broken. The spirit of poverty and bondage is broken in the name of Jesus. Poverty, the spirit of lack and want is broken off you now in the name of Jesus. Prophesy to your finances that money shall come to you in Jesus name. Money will chase you down in the name of Jesus and you shall have rest for your soul. The Lord says, you shall know heaven on earth. As it is in heaven so shall it be in your life. Open heavens in Jesus name!*

The spirit of weariness is broken off your life because with the anointing of God there is no weariness in Jesus name. Things God wanted to do but because you have not flowed in the anointing the enemy has fought your vision. He has stopped your prosperity and he's put you in distress and bondage but through the Lord you shall break the yoke of bondage. Every spirit of determent to things that God has promised you that you have not seen shall come to pass! The prayer and decree that determent and bondage is broken in Jesus name. The blood of Jesus prevails. Every spirit that has tried to hold you back is broken. It is your time to be oiled up!

Mending Christ's Body

In a dream Ambassador Gwyneth saw a white wall, at the end of the white wall she saw the hand of God sewing together prayer cloths. The Lord said to tell His leaders that some of the church has become like a whitewashed tomb, like a whitewashed wall. When they come together as pastors and leaders then they will see revival but because some of the church has become like the Mafia they are not walking in unity and loving one another. Ministering in many pastor's conferences around the world they see many things that are happening in these meetings much like the world and even like the Mafia. The Lord told her in the dream that He wants her to address this issue of unity within the body of Christ.

She had a dream and saw a group of bishops and elders they were standing on the right side of her. On the left side of her she could see another group of bishops, leaders and elders rising to the top going up the mountain. The vehicle carrying the pastors turned over. The bishops and pastors there on the right side she knew each of them, but their motives were evil. These bishops, pastors, and church members came against the other pastors in the accident. As the car turned over she floated over to them, she opened the rear door to help the pastor who had been hurt in the accident. The pastor was so light, he was wrapped in a blanket. When she reached in to pick him up and take him out of the car he was fragile because he'd been hurt in the accident. When she looked down she began to carry him wrapped in this blanket. From a far-off she saw a hospital for pastors and bishops. Her heart and motive were to take him to the hospital. As she was going she looked down and the blanket in her arms had turned into a large yellow business envelope. Written on the envelope were names of pastors, leaders and bishops. Some had been crossed off by the other bishops and church members with a black marker. They had been black listed. Some of the names were pastors and leaders that she knew. As she held the envelope it began to move, and she pulled out a foot from the envelope that had been severed from the ankle. Then she pulled out a hand that had been cut from the wrist. She took the envelope with her as she floated to this hospital emergency room for pastors.

As she entered she told them about the car accident. They said to her you need to see the head of this hospital. She left the emergency room and went to the other end of the hospital. The Man in charge came to the counter. He told her that He needed her to help Him with this project of bringing unity and healing to the Body of Christ. The Man over the hospital represented the Lord. He said to her that the pastors and leaders are cutting each other's hands and feet off. There is a spiritual assassination taking place because of competitive jealousy.

The Word of God says how lovely on the mountain are the feet of them who bring good news, Isaiah 52:7. However, the church members, and bishops are cutting each other's ministries off. The Lord told her in the dream for her to tell the leaders how lovely on the mountain are the feet of them who bring good news. He said that my church is cutting off each other's hands. The hand represents covenant and it is used to make agreements. The hand helps to heal. The hand is the apostle;

the prophet who points the way; the evangelist; the pastor; and the teacher. He said but they have all fought each other and become like the Mafia in the church with a hit list for each other. He told her to tell the church that they are wounding each other. If they come together as one, they can take nations for Christ (John 17:21). They can take cities for the kingdom of God and for the Lord.

The first time the Lord took her into the Holy of Holies during a five-hour vision was after she left a pastor's meeting. In the pastor's meeting people spoke about what was happening within their ministry for that week. They shared their victories and some of the difficulties. One of the pastor's said that at his church they were voting in new leadership. The old administration was leaving, and a new administration was coming. He said, two pastors came into this meeting, one had on a long trench coat with a rifle underneath and the other pastor had a 45 pistol in his pocket. This is a Pentecostal church. The pastor went on to say that the opposing side burned down the church of the other. Ambassador Gwyneth said to the pastor facilitating the meeting, "Do you expect me to believe this Pentecostal pastor would burn down someone else's church?" She said, "Do you expect me to believe that pastors would come to church with guns and rifles?" He said to her, "Do you know that a pastor was shot dead in the pulpit?" In his eyes she was naïve.

She went home and cried. She cried, wept, and cried until her eyes were red and her stomach was aching. She said, God if this is your church, if pastors are fighting other pastors and they're talking about other evangelists. They're pulling down other bishops; and members are talking about each other. How is the Body of Christ going to have an awakening? How are they going to have revival? This is God's church even today. As she wept, the Lord took her into the Holy of Holies and she understood Ezekiel's vision when he went into the Holy of Holies and saw the Shekinah glory. She could see the wheel within the wheel, and the cherubim around the throne of God. The angels were singing around the throne of God in a melodious sound. As she wept she said, "God these are your people, your leaders. Why would they want to cut each other's feet off? Cut each other's hand off?" Only one thing that she understood within those five hours in English, the Lord said to her and she believes it's for the church. He said, "You shall do greater works. You shall do greater works than I" John 14:12. The Body of Christ does not see the greater works in the church because of the fighting and division. God is waiting on His church to arise. He is waiting on His church to come together in unity. Not competing with each other but complementing each other.

When Ambassador Gwyneth was in Japan the Lord gave her a dream. When she arrived in Korea she asked the Korean women to cut these prayer cloths that she saw in the dream. She said to every bishop, and pastor that is willing to fast, not food, but to fast their words from talking about each other and from pulling down each other. She asked them to sign this cloth. She told the pastors in pastor's and bishop's meeting that if they're not willing to bring unity to the Body of Christ, if they're not willing to fast their words and gossip against each other causing division, she asked them not to sign it and not even to pray over it. Churches are empty because the enemy has come in to divide, to conquer, and to pull people down - to say, "Look at that person's gift, I would have done it this way instead." When the church comes together just like at Azusa Street, God shows up and manifests His glory. At Azusa every tribe attended, every nation, and every continent came to the revival at 312 Azusa Street. All of the Holy Spirit's gifts were in operation.

Reconciliation

In Tulsa Oklahoma they recently enacted a policy to include the history of the 1921 Greenwood race riot in the history books within the public schools. Bishop Clark was a survivor of this race riot. Before he went to heaven, Bishop Clark was the oldest living survivor of the race riot and his daughter and grand-daughter, Ambassadors Gwyneth and Star have written about it in his autobiography, *His Story, History and His Secret.*

It's not about reparations but it is about reconciliation. Ambassadors Gwyneth and Star could spend their whole life saying their grandparents' house was burned down by the white man, their great grandparents' home was burned down by the white man, their dad's stepdad was burned up by the white man. They could say the white man owes them. God is about reconciliation no matter what has happened. Some of their culture has the mentality of God damn America and they want to go back to Africa because of what the white man has done. They believe their dad lived to be 109 years old because he knew how to love. He knew how to come together in unity despite what happened to him.

> *Despite what pastor, leader or tribe has wronged you, know that God is a God of recompense. When we hold our peace, God will fight our battles. The greatest witness of the Azusa Street outpouring was nations and ethnicities coming together. We need that type of reconciliation in the Azusa Now. We want to blame others. It does not matter the color of your skin, God wants us to reconcile in love. He holds the king's heart and will direct it like a watercourse. Then you can walk in the favor of God.*

The first year that Ambassador Star was in the Miss Oklahoma USA pageant she was second place. An older African American who was in her 70's said, "Let's go. They didn't give that crown to her because she's black." Sometimes it has nothing to do with skin color. The next year when Star returned she won first place, and the crown. It was significant because it was 100 years from the year that Bishop Clark was born in Oklahoma, Indian Territory. His granddaughter becomes Miss Oklahoma 100 years from the year he was born in Oklahoma. Oklahoma had the worst race riot in history. Bishop Clark's mother and grandparents' home was burned down. His step-father was killed in the riot, but reconciliation and forgiveness were important for them to teach.

See how God fights for His people and see how He brings a great recompense of reward. Nations, tribes, and cultures have been wronged in some way, though the enemy make them feel like they are the only ones. If the church cuts each other's feet and hands off, if tribes, colors, and nations fight against each other, Satan has won. That's why the Lord said, tell the church they have become like a whitewash wall. He said they must come together.

When Ambassador Gwyneth and Star were departing Tanzania for Kenya, a Kenyan man sat across from them, a Christian man. He saw Ambassador Gwyneth reading the Bible. He made conversation with her about the Word of God. She told him that they were excited about going to Kenya. They told him that they waited after the presidential elections because of potential instability within the nation during the elections. They told him while waiting that the visa had expired for Kenya, and they had stayed and ministered in Uganda during that time. The intention was to come after the holiday Jamhuri Day. The day that they were going to swear in Raila Odinga and they were instructed to go when there was peace.

After they had discussed this the man said, "Yeah, the reason we didn't fight this election was because we were unprepared." He said, "We didn't have our guns but in five years if this place has to be like Rwanda it will happen." He said, "Look at Rwanda now, there is peace." He said, "If one million people must die, it will happen. I know how to fight, I was a sergeant in the Kenyan army and I am tired of what's been stolen from me and I'm going to get it back. I'm tired of black colonization." Ambassador Gwyneth was surprised by the conversation of this person who confessed Christ. How can the Body of Christ have an awakening with this type of mind set?

> *If we're not unified, and if we don't love, we could be in church and still within our hearts carry a lot of hatred. You can be like the bishops that assassinate other bishops.*

In 2016, Ambassadors Gwyneth and Star had 12 to 14 pastors and bishops in America tell them, "I hate white people." It's cultural. That's why the church must come together. The church must be one, John 17:21.

Forgiveness

When they went to South Korea some people were burning the Japanese flag. They were burning pictures of the Japanese president because the Japanese killed millions of Koreans and Chinese. Every country Ambassadors Gwyneth and Star have visited they see the enemy using the same strategy - divide and conquer especially within the church. So that it cannot prosper. So that the church cannot have an awakening. So that the church will not have a revival. They went to a meeting that was led by a spirit-filled Jewish woman.

Right before the prayer meeting began they were taking prayer requests and out of the leader's heart she said, "I hate the Germans." When Ambassador Gwyneth grew up she was told all policemen are pigs. She was told white people are blonde haired blue-eyed devils. Someone told Ambassador Gwyneth they can't get a job because they were black and the white man was holding them back. Just like they told Ambassador Star, "You can't win Miss Oklahoma because you're black."

> *Let everyone examine their own heart. What is in the heart that is preventing us from receiving the fullness. What traditions? What have you been taught in your culture? Some cultures may think they are superior to others. That is the definition of prejudice. It is where we prejudge others. No matter where you've been or where you are going we must be unified. Some cultures often blame the other culture for their problems. No one can hold you back. No one can hold you down. Regardless of your socioeconomic background or the color of your skin.*

Some people do not understand that a large portion of black culture in Tanzania Tippu Tip an African sold many other Africans as slaves. He sold kings and heads of tribes to the Arabs, and later to the Europeans. Some went into the United States.

Instead of loving one another the enemy wants to rip the Body of Christ apart. However, believers are better together. The Body of Christ needs one another to succeed. It's like charcoal, when it's lit by the fire to cook the meat and it's turned the charcoal gets red hot then it gets white hot. The same within the church with the fire of the Holy Spirit, if each person has dynamite whole cities can be won for the Lord. If one person has a stick of dynamite and another person has a stick of dynamite and the church lights their dynamite together in unity serious damage can happen to the kingdom of darkness. Nations, cities, and communities can be possessed for the kingdom of God.

Bishop Clark was a survivor of the 1921 Tulsa race riot. During speaking engagements, he always spoke about love that's why when he would walk in a room people would see a glow around him. They would see a light around him. It was the anointing.

Someone said that in Rwanda there was a group of people who came to the altar every day to repent of things they knew that they did and things they did not know, and the people would have a shine and glow about them. They called it the Shining Church. That is the anointing that stays upon the lives. Even in finances, breakthrough in finances come when the Word of the Lord is obeyed by giving. What leaves the hand does not leave the life, but it enters the future multiplied. The enemy does not want believers to release but to hold on in fear and unforgiveness. Many are going to church, but God is calling His people to change and be different. After reading the Bible, God wants there to be a change of heart. Let the love of God toward one another manifest and follow Him in all His ways. Obedience to the command of the Lord is better than sacrifice.

> *God was sorry He made Saul king when he turned his back from following Him. We want the blessings of God not to turn from us. Do you desire God's blessing? We don't want God to say I'm sorry.*

The Lord said that Saul had not performed His commandments. Even Samuel was grieved after he appointed Saul as king. God wants His people to be repentant. He wants holiness and maturity in His children. Maturity brings about the anointing of God. In the Greek perfect is translated mature. After Samuel anointed Saul, Samuel had to tell Saul everything that he was to do. When he anointed Saul, he said, "Everything you touch will be blessed - the blessings will follow you." He said, "Whatever you do it will be blessed." That was before Saul turned his back on God. That was before the partial obedience.

When the children of God stay under the anointing of God everything they touch and everything they do will be blessed. When Saul was anointed the Word of God says, Saul prophesied as the spirit and the anointing of God came upon him. After he turned his back the Word of God says that there was regret because he didn't stay humble and he didn't stay small in his own eyes. He became big in his own eyes, he did his own mission and did not obey what he was supposed to do. Let the church believe for a greater awakening and the presence of God by forgiving others and being obedient.

Righteousness Exalts

This next move of God is a movement of holiness. However, there is a movement that says believers don't have to obey the word of God. Some believe that everyone in the church is going to sin anyway and no one can live holy. They believe people should do what they want to do because Jesus has already died for their sins. Some say that no one can live holy, people can do what they want because God's grace covers. They say, "We can do whatever we want to do and still go to heaven." If the church believes that they have become disobedient to the word of God and He will remove His presence and His anointing from them.

> *If we believe we cannot live holy it is as if we are saying the blood of Jesus is not good enough. We're saying the blood of Jesus is not powerful enough to keep us holy. It's like saying the blood of Jesus is not powerful enough to help us live a repented life. We're saying the Holy Spirit and the fire of God cannot burn the sin out of our lives. God is saying church when you live holy, when you live righteous, when you live repentant, the Holy Spirit and the glory of God will be upon your lives. You will not only see visitations of His presence, but the Holy Spirit and His glory will be a habitation among you. When you return to holiness there will be a habitation of His presence. Believe that God can keep you saved, sanctified and set apart for His use.*

Frist Samuel 15:22 says "Obedience is better than sacrifice." When believers obey God, they will not lose their heirship. When they obey they can walk in the divine blessings of God and be kings and priests unto the Lord. In this passage the Lord is speaking of Saul and He rejects Saul. Does the Lord delight in burnt offerings and sacrifices as much as in obeying the Lord? To obey is better than sacrifice and to heed is better than the fat of rams. Rebellion is a sin is witchcraft. Stubbornness is an iniquity and becomes idolatry. "You reject the Lord and you are rejected as King Saul." Many times, the church fails to teach Scripture that says God is a God of correction, convincing, and rebuking (2 Timothy 3:16;4:2; Hebrews 12:5,6).

God corrects His sons and daughters so that they can be under the anointing. God wants to His people but sometimes that rebellious spirit comes and the anointing leaves. 1 Samuel 10:6, "The spirit of the Lord will come upon you, and you will prophesy with them and be turned into another man."

> *Pray that the anointing will always stay with us. You will prophesy with them and you will be changed to a different person. How many want that transformation, to be a different person. The Spirit of the Lord will come powerfully upon you and you will prophesy with them and you will be changed. This was the opportunity Saul had before he became king. We believe today that you will be that changed person and that everything your hands find to do will be blessed. You will do everything according to the will of God with a repentant heart.*

> *When you are anointed with God it leads to a radical departure from the nominal Christian life. You're not normal or nominal but a peculiar people set apart unto the Lord. When anointing comes upon your life you depart from nominal Christianity. As you cry out to the Lord and seek His face and not His hand you walk into the divine blessings God has for you. People may think you're radical, abnormal, weird, or strange but*

> *God is waiting for the phenomenal. He wants to raise you up as a radical Christian with the Holy Spirit and the fire of God. Not killing and wounding others but bringing light and revival to a dark world. With obedience to walk in the divine anointing that God has for you. He's wanting and waiting for radical Christians to arise.*

What is a phenomenon, it means strange occurrences. That is the phenomenal. A radical Christianity is arising where people are not going to be afraid to talk about Jesus. Why will Muslims strap bombs to their chest and blow themselves up for what they believe? God is saying for the true church, Christianity with the Holy Spirit and the fire of God, to arise.

Ambassador Star began preaching at eight years old and she was baptized in the Holy Spirit at three years old speaking in tongues. Let's start raising up our children and training them to go to their schools and pray for the sick to get well. They'll go to the schools and witness to their teachers because the Lord is waiting on the church to arise. The church is hiding and has become appeasing wanting more to be liked than to be obedient. He wants all to have backbone, and to be courageous, to be warriors, to be radical and to take the head off the uncircumcised Philistine. He wants the church to use the sword of the Spirit to influence government, and to influence media. He wants the church to influence in areas like education, and business. However, the church is trying to appease men and be liked instead of pleasing God. Therefore, becoming disobedient to the things of God. Afraid to say, "Yes I have the Holy Spirit, and yes I speak in tongues." He's waiting on men and women of God to arise with the anointing of God upon their lives to take their kingship. Saul was more concerned about what the people thought about him then what God thought about him, 1 Samuel 15:24. So, he lost his kingship. He was disobedient because of the opinion of man and forfeited his kingship.

Ambassador Gwyneth is not concerned with what people think about her or to be liked. She is here to preach the unadulterated Word of God. So that the church may be awakened and arise in the power of the Holy Spirit and not like pussycats saying "meow, meow, meow." May the church of the living God arise and roar boldly like a lion. He is waiting for men and women to rise and roar like lions with courage not shrinking back in fear. Many are complacent that is one of the reasons the church hasn't seen the awakening.

> *It is not about others opinion of you, but it is about the price you must pay to be under the anointing of God.*

It's time to wake up and take over. It's not time to take sides, it is time for the church of the living God to arise in the power of the Holy Spirit and the anointing of God. So that signs, wonders, miracles will be evident, and auditoriums, stadiums and churches would be filled with the glory of God. That is the anointing, that is the ability to be able to have the supernatural power to do the will of God.

> *My prayer for you today is that you would be bold as lions. That you would rise like Jesus the Lion of Judah and possess your nations, your cities, your communities, your family and villages with the power of the Holy Spirit and for kingdom of God. We pray that the Holy Spirit's power of God would burn within your heart.*

The Greatest Miracle

Prayer of Salvation: Confess with your mouth and believe in your heart-

"God I confess that I have sinned against You. Forgive me. I believe that Jesus Christ died on the cross for my sins, and He rose from the dead on the third day. Lord Jesus I accept You as Savior and Lord of my life. I surrender my will and rights over to Your will. Holy Spirit fill me with your power and presence. I believe that from this moment I am a new creation. The old has passed away and all things have become new."

If you prayed this prayer from your heart, you have now stepped into new life in Christ. Please let someone know of your decision and write us too letting us know your decision for Christ. You are now part of God's family! 2 Corinthians 5:17

Write to:
Life Enrichment Ministries
P.O. Box 2717
Tulsa, OK 74101 USA

Email: admin@lemglobal.org
Call: +1-918-288-0400
WhatsApp: +1-918-409-7700
Website www.lemglobal.org

Watch our 24 Hour Online TV channel by logging on worldwide at any time:
www.lemglobal.org
DRGWYNANDSTAR.COM
YouTube: Dr. Gwyn and Star

Other Books, Study Courses, Seminars, Training, and Leadership Manuals

- Azusa Outpouring: Unleashing the Holy Spirit, Signs, Wonders, and Miracles, Second Edition 8/2018, 205 pgs. (LEMIT School Curriculum): ISBN 978-1-949594-02-7 (Available in Spanish: 978-1-949594-00-3 112 pgs. & Portuguese 978-1-949594-03-4, 117 pgs.)
- Get in the Go: A Guide to Short-Term Missions, Second Edition, 9/2018: (LEMIT School Curriculum): ISBN 978-1-949594-04-1, 150 pgs.
- Lifestyles for a Lifetime Health: Your Ultimate Health & Wellness Guidebook, Second Edition, 7/2018 (LEMIT School Curriculum): ISBN 978-1-949594-01-0, 134 pgs.
- Live, Hope & Dream Again: Overcoming Rejection and Failure, 9/2018 (Set Apart/LEMIT School Curriculum): ISBN 978-1-949594-05-8, 150 pgs.
- His Story, History, and His Secret: Life Through the Eyes of Bishop Otis Grandville Clark, Second Edition, 9/2018: ISBN 978-1-949594-06-5, 125 pgs.
- A New Wave of Refreshing for the Nations Kingdoms, 10/2006: ISBN 978-1-425909-34-5, 160 pgs.

To Order copies of any of these books, manuals and training material write to:
Life Enrichment Ministries, P.O. Box 2717, Tulsa, OK 74101 USA.
Or call (in the USA) 918-288-0400 or +1-918-288-0400 (outside the USA).
Email us at admin@lemglobal.org

All Resources available at www.Amazon.com and everywhere books are sold.

Order today, Book Sales help support LEMGlobal.org World Missions.

Partnership with a Global Ministry

LEM has a world-wide mission to ignite and spread the flames of the Great Awakening. They carry the DNA of the Azusa Street Revival throughout the nation and the world. Imparting the gifts of the Holy Spirit with signs, wonders, healings, and miracles.

Celebrating more than 32 years of international missions, apostolic, and world evangelism, Dr. Gwyneth, and Amb. Star have just laid the groundwork for great things ahead. They are carrying revival fire of the Holy Spirit to the Church, Media, Arts & Entertainment, Business, Government, Family, and Education.

They carry the actual and prophetic Power-of-Attorney from the Azusa Street Revival, passed to them by their Dad, Bishop Otis G. Clark who attended the original Azusa Street Mission and was mentored by the founding members.

Bishop Clark's assignment was to continue the legacy of the Azusa International Mission. For Over 90 years he faithfully carried the torch, and power of the Holy Spirit around the world until the age of 109 years young. He preached on a Sunday and went home to be with the Lord on the Monday before Pentecost. Dr. Gwyneth & Amb. Star carry as the next generation the apostolic and prophetic mantle. Their mandate is to see the church unleashed and walking in holiness, power, signs, wonders, miracles, and healings - unleashing the Holy Spirit within them.

They are blessed to travel all over the world ministering and preaching the Good News. Missions and outreach has taken them to several countries including Argentina; Costa Rica; Mexico; Uruguay; Colombia; Brazil; Canada; England; Wales; Netherlands; Spain; France; Japan; Singapore; Malaysia; China; Korea; Taiwan; Haiti; Jamaica; Bahamas; South Africa; Lesotho; Mozambique; Uganda;

Tanzania; Kenya; Zimbabwe; Egypt; Israel and more. They are Contending for an Awakening and releasing the Azusa Apostolic Faith of the Holy Spirit!

Our Vision is to reach the world with the Gospel of Jesus Christ through teaching, preaching, and training; and bring truth and restoration to the Body of Christ through the Word of God.

Our Mission is to Save Souls; Love God & People; Heal Hurts; Equip Workers; and Send disciples into all the world to preach the Good News and make disciples of all nations, baptizing them in the name of the Father and of the Son and of the Holy Spirit, in Jesus name and teaching them to obey everything Christ Jesus commanded. Matthew 28:18-19. The Great Commission is our mission.

We are an evangelistic organization that accomplishes the will of our Father through Teaching, Speaking, Preaching, Business Consulting, Ministry Training School, and Evangelism/Outreach.

Partner with us financially and through prayer. When you sow into Life Enrichment Ministries you are sowing into rich soil. Get involved with advancing the Kingdom of God and help us "Bring Life & Light to businesses, homes, & Ministries coast to coast & around the world."

Write or send check to:
Life Enrichment Ministries
P.O. Box 2717
Tulsa, OK 74101
Email: admin@lemglobal.org
Call: +1-918-288-0400
WhatsApp: +1-918-409-7700

Donate: www.paypal.me/lemglobal

Cash App: $lemglobal

Visit or donate securely online at our Website www.lemglobal.org

Watch our 24 Hour Online TV channel by logging on worldwide at any time: www.lemglobal.org

Life Enrichment Ministerial Association

Mandate: "Bring Life & Light to Businesses, Homes & Ministries Coast to Coast and Around the World"

The Life Enrichment Ministerial Association of Christian Churches, leaders and Ministries, was birthed out of a divine mandate given to its founder and president, Dr. Gwyneth Williams. Dr. Williams carried the call of God for an organization that would serve as a vital force in the Body of Christ for the training, equipping, and releasing of churches and ministries within God's people so that they would impact nations. It is a multi-cultural network of diverse leaders in ministry and marketplace that desire mentoring, covering, and apostolic impartation.

To facilitate this effort towards equipping, God directed Dr. Williams to start a traveling ministry, Life Enrichment Incorporated, in 1984 and to begin ministering in a variety of churches and conferences throughout the world. The evangelical mantel upon Dr. Williams life is evident through her extensive writings on training short-term missionaries in the local church, training hundreds of missionary evangelists, and facilitating mission teams to thirty-three countries (many more than once) and five continents.

Dr. Williams was the pastor and founder of The Azusa Mission—a daily inner city outreach in Seattle, Washington; and the Christian bookstore for pastors and leaders. The Azusa Mission transported the homeless from shelters every week to The Azusa Mission where they were provided with the Word of God, a hot meal, new clothes, and groceries. The homeless weren't the only ones attracted to The Azusa Mission, but many local ministers and pastors called The Azusa Mission their home church. Out of the overwhelming community response, over 22 pastors and ministers were ordained by Life Enrichment Ministerial Association and today thousands of pastors, leaders and organizations have been positively impacted by Life Enrichment Ministries through Mentorship, Ordination, Licensure, Certification, Training and Consultation. And LEMA is ready to partner with you.

Life Enrichment Ministerial Association Membership Includes but not limited to:*
- One LEMIT college course ($300 value-excluding books) with Certificate upon completion
- Missions training manual ($25 value)
- Exclusive access to LEM Mission trips, Seminars, and Building Godly & Healthy Relationship Cruises with 15% discount ($300-$500 value)
- Missions Training and mentorship with educated, experienced & qualified staff
- Prayer journal ($15 value)
- Annual LEM team member T-shirt ($15 value)
- Annual Membership card
- Annual Membership certificate
- Fee: Yearly membership fee $550 payable one time or $50 per month for 12 months.*Membership benefits & fees are subject to change.

Benefits of joining LEMA: Ministry Covering & Empowerment; Renewed Vision for your ministry; Training, mentorship & equipping; Missions, Outreach & Practicum experience; Certification; Ministerial identification & credentials; Inspiration, fellowship, encouragement; and Refreshment body, mind and spirit;

We are a Membership organization empowering & equipping the body of Christ for the work of the ministry. We are not a denomination; however, we license and ordain ministers who desire to be covered and trained for the work of full-time and part-time ministry and who meet the application requirements.

To join LEMA please write to us at LEMA, POB 2717, Tulsa, OK 74101 USA or complete the online Form to begin the application process at www.lemglobal.org, look for LEMA.

LEMIT

School of Missions & Theology

Life Enrichment School of Missions & Theology is the fulfillment of a dream God planted in our founder's heart - Dr. Gwyneth Williams years ago: a dream to see His children firmly established in the Word and equipped to do the work of the ministry. It is for the mentoring, training and equipping of the saints for the work of ministry in conjunction with the World-Wide Missions Outreach initiatives.

LEMIT is being raised up to prepare a new generation of fully equipped believers to effectively do the work of the ministry, whether this ministry is through the local church, through para-church structure, or through independent ministry. Our mission is to provide quality Biblical, theological, and practical ministry training for all believers world-wide.

Many will enroll in LEMIT to deepen their knowledge of God's Word. Others will enroll to become better equipped for doing ministry through the local church. Still others will enroll to begin preparation for full-time ministry.

Is God calling you to strengthen your knowledge of His word? Is He calling you to make a difference in a hurting world? If so, I want to strongly encourage you to submit your application for admission to Life Enrichment School of Missions & Theology. Join us and learn how to minister in the love and power of the Holy Spirit through the anointed teaching of a Spirit-filled faculty. Short 12 week or intensive two week courses are available; full or part time; online, seminar and correspondence. Certification and Diplomas available in Missions, Counseling,

Biblical Studies, Church Administration, Leadership, Christian Education, Practical Ministry, Health & Wellness, and Godly Relationships.

I am excited about what God is doing and going to do in your life as you prepare and further equip yourself for servant hood in His Kingdom.

Why you should be a part of Life Enrichment School of Missions and Theology:
- World ministry opportunities through our internship program
- Partnership with a ministry linked directly to the Azusa Street Revival and Bishop Otis Clark, Father of Modern Day Pentecost.
- Sound Teaching with faith based emphasis.
- Practical training and spiritual growth.
- Intensive ministry and biblical seminars.
- Help with placement and recommendations into ministries after graduation

LEMIT Courses Offered: Old Testament, New Testament, Signs & Wonders, Holy Spirit in the Now, Life of Paul, Evangelism, Ministry Practicum, Principles & Patterns of Divine Healing, Discipleship & Small Groups, Hebrews & General Epistles, Israel Study Tour, Luke & Acts, Christian Faith & Ministry, Christian Caregiving, Faith & Human Development, Ministry & Leadership Development, Pre-Marital Counseling, Marriage & Family, History of Christianity I & II, Prayer, Principles of Biblical Counseling, Youth Ministry, Crisis Management, Church Administration, Adult Ministry, Life of Christ, Spiritual Issues in Substance Abuse, Major World Religions, Theology & Practice of Spiritual Warfare, Christian Missions, Sermon Preparation, Ministry Internship, Practices of Health & Wellness, Godly Relationships, And much more!

LEMIT Online School Of Ministry Open Enrollment: Enroll any Monday for Mentorship, missions, training, discipleship, and intern opportunities! Enroll today for Life Enrichment School of teaching and training in the five-fold ministry; it is one of the major aspects of the Azusa Outreach, for the perfecting of the saints Ephesians 4:12.

LEMIT is Continuing the "Winning Legacy" through Training. They continue to preach, teach, and train the Body, they are seeing a strengthening of the local church in tremendous ways. Lives are being saved; saints are being emboldened for the work of the Lord; and others are receiving the Baptism of the Holy Spirit and fire.

Enroll today:
Life Enrichment Ministries
P.O. Box 2717
Tulsa, OK 74101
Email: admin@lemglobal.org
Call: +1-918-288-0400
WhatsApp: +1-918-409-7700
Visit our Website www.lemglobal.org,
Select: Training – School of Missions & Theology
Online Courses available 24 Hours by logging on worldwide at any time:
www.lemglobal.org
DRGWYNANDSTAR.COM
YouTube: Dr. Gwyn and Star

If your organization, ministry, college, university, business or church would like to invite Dr. Gwyneth, and Ambassador Star for speaking, impartation, mentoring, leadership coaching, and/or to organize a LEMIT seminar/course or conference for your workers, leaders, staff, ministers, employees, employers, congregation, youth and young adults, contact us through the above information.

Mandate: "Bring Life & Light to Businesses, Homes & Ministries Coast to Coast and Around the World"

Partnership

If you share in the vision and passion of Life Enrichment Ministries to take the gospel to the nations and would like to join us as a partner in ministry, we invite you to contribute in whatever manner is most convenient for you: one-time or monthly. As an organization 100% of our income is donation based. Every gift makes a difference. You can make a secure, online donation with your bank card, or by sending us a check through the mail. May you experience God's richest blessings as you give according to His divine will for your life.

Write or send check to:
Life Enrichment Ministries
P.O. Box 2717
Tulsa, OK 74101

Email: admin@lemglobal.org
Call: +1-918-288-0400
WhatsApp: +1-918-409-7700
Donate: www.paypal.me/lemglobal
Cash App: $lemglobal
Visit or donate securely online at our Website www.lemglobal.org

Watch our 24 Hour Online TV channel by logging on worldwide at any time:
www.lemglobal.org
DRGWYNANDSTAR.COM
YouTube: Dr. Gwyn and Star

About the Authors

Bishop Otis G. Clark
"Azusa Street Direct Link"

Bishop Otis G. Clark was born on February 13, 1903, in Meridian, Oklahoma before Oklahoma even a state. At the time it was Indian Territory. At the age of eighteen, Clark was caught in the "1921 Tulsa Race Riot" in the Greenwood District of Tulsa, Oklahoma. At the time Greenwood was a mecca for African-Americans who owned their own successful businesses due to the oil boom. This riot was one of the worse race riots on American soil caused by jealously. As a young man fleeing for his life he hoboed on a train to California looking for his biological father and left Tulsa for many years.

Clark was heavily involved with the original Azusa Street Mission members. The Azusa Street Revival began in 1906 and was led by William J. Seymour in Los

Angeles, California. Before the Azusa Street Mission building was torn down, Clark was given the Power of Attorney by Bishop Driscoll over the Azusa Street Mission. Samuel M. Crouch of Los Angeles, California officially ordained Clark as a preacher - this took place at 33rd and Compton Street in Los Angeles. He also had the honor of serving Charles H. Mason, whom he affectionately called "Dad." Bishop Mason is the founder of the Church of God in Christ.

While living in California, Clark had the opportunity to rub shoulders with many famous actors. He knew a young man named Steppin' Fetchit. Steppin' Fetchit chose Clark to be a friend and buddy. Clark had the opportunity to serve Clark Gable, Joan Crawford and Charley Chaplin, some of America's most prominent movie stars. Clark and his wife lived in Joan Crawford's home. He was the butler and she was the cook.

The years of 1929-1932 represented dark and desperate days for America, known as The Great Depression. In the midst of the chaos of this time - God blessed Clark. During The Great Depression he was well provided for with ample food and clothing. Not once did he stand in a bread or soup line.

To the glory of God, he served as an International Minister for over 90 years, longer than the average life expectancy. He was known as the "World's Oldest Traveling Minister." Clark went home on May 21, 2012 at 109 years. He was going strong as he continued to preach up until the day before he went home to be with the Lord. Clark's daughter, Dr. Gwyneth Williams and grand-daughter, Ambassador Star Williams are carrying on the torch of revival and his Azusa Street Revival legacy. They continue to preach and write about the oracles of God. To read more about his life – order Bishop Clark's biography, His Story, History & His Secret today at www.lemglobal.org

Interesting Facts:
- Evangelist Clark was older than the state of Oklahoma, which was incorporated in 1907.
- He knew original members of the Azusa Street Mission, which was started by William J. Seymour in 1906 and was given the power of attorney of the original Azusa Street
- He was the oldest living survivor of the 1921 Tulsa Race Riot. This took place on America's Black Wall street, the Greenwood district of Tulsa, OK.
- He cared for himself independently
- He took no medications
- He had all his natural teeth, no dentures
- He did not regularly wear glasses with the exception of reading glasses
- He ate a healthy and balanced diet of lean beef, chicken, fruits and vegetables
- He threw out the ceremonial first pitch for the Boston Red Sox the year they won the World Series
- He traveled on missions to Africa. The first when he was 103 yrs. old and the second when he was 104 yrs. old and went to the West Indies at 107 and England at 108 years.
- He was the world's oldest traveling minister
- He attended the second World's Fair in 1933 in Chicago, IL...and guess what they previewed?...The TELEVISION!

Dr. Gwyneth Williams

Dr. Gwyneth Williams is a mother, author, blogger, international evangelist, and business consultant. She is the daughter of Bishop Otis G. Clark. She is the mother of one daughter, Star Williams, who is Miss Global Ambassador, a Miss Oklahoma USA and top ten in the Miss USA Pageant.

Williams earned a Doctor of Ministry Degree in 1996, and a Master of Divinity in 1989, both from Oral Roberts University in Tulsa, Oklahoma. In 1984, she received a Bachelor of Science Degree in accounting, specializing in for-profit and non-profit accounting. She did her undergraduate work at Indiana State University, Indiana Central College and Martin University.

Her professional experience is vast. She is co-founder, along with Bishop Otis Clark, of Life Enrichment Ministries Azusa with a Holiness Mission. She has been the Chief Executive Officer of Life Enrichment Inc. since 1986. Dr. Gwyneth's work experience encompasses major positions pertaining to education, consulting, pastoring and leadership. Her administrative and leadership skills consist of overseeing the organization's missions, publishing, seminars, training, financial and budget development. She's written numerous grants proposals, polity charts, business plans, evaluations, and organizational assessments.

She held the title of Field Education and Intern Program supervisor where she trained numerous graduate and undergraduate students in the school of business, education, and theology. She's trained workers for thirty-two years in the Life Enrichment Missions Training program for overseas internships throughout dozens of nations. She's had the responsibility of educating many students who received training and certification in theology and missions. Training included cultural sensitivity; foreign relations; historical, theological, and practical training; such as training nationals in music, home economics, nursing and hygiene, counseling, communication, drama, adult and youth ministry, and carpentry.

She was a pastor for seven years in Seattle, Washington ministering to the homeless and down and out. She is a dynamic pastor, apostle, preacher and evangelist. The ministry has ordained and trained over 300 pastors and ministers under Life Enrichment Ministerial Association. Additionally, she lived in England while studying the culture, writing curriculum, and researching for a faith-based ministry. She's authored seven books. Her heart is to see the Power of the Holy Spirit unleashed within the Body of Christ with Signs, wonders, and miracles following; and minister, pastors, and leaders released in their calling as they walk in the Fullness of God.

Her life mission is to "Bring Light and Life to Businesses, Homes, and Ministries, Coast to Coast and Around the World." She has ministered, trained and evangelized in more than thirty-two countries. Her greatest joy is to see the body of Christ empowered and equipped with the power of the Holy Spirit. She is honored to continue the legacy of her father, Bishop Clark, and carry the anointing of Azusa to the nations.

Ambassador Star Williams

Star is the daughter of Dr. Gwyneth Williams and the grand-daughter of Bishop Otis G. Clark. She is the Vice-President & Director for Life Enrichment Ministries Azusa with a Holiness Mission. She is a published author, blogger, TV & radio personality, international speaker, preacher, purity ambassador and mentor. She is an ordained minister and full-time servant of Jesus Christ.

While living in England she studied Broadcast Journalism and English Literature for one year. Star graduated with a degree in Communications from Oral Roberts University. She graduated Magna Cum Laude. She is Miss Global Ambassador, a perpetual title bestowed upon her in 2016. She is a former Miss Oklahoma USA, and Top 10 in the Miss USA pageant. In addition, she held the title of Miss Black Oklahoma and was 1st runner up to Miss Black International.

Star has working along-side her mother and grand-father since a small girl traveling, ministering side by side to over thirty-two. She's been writing since the age of 12 and preaching since the age of 8. She served the homeless in the Azusa Mission church in Seattle Washington for five years while pastoring the youth group.

Star enjoys reading, exercising, spending time with family, and meeting new people. She hosts a radio broadcast entitled Building Godly & Healthy Relationships. On BGHR she equips people to live out their Christian faith, being as shining lights for Jesus. Star affirms Jeremiah 29:11 and Matthew 6:33 and strongly believes that God has great plans for every person that is fulfilled through seeking the Lord Jesus first. Follow and subscribe to her podcast at www.lemglobal.org

She has a passion for the nations of the world and young adult ministry. Star inspires youth and adults alike that once you give your life to Jesus, He can and will keep you through a committed relationship with Him. She passionately believes in the keeping power of the Holy Spirit (1 Cor. 1:8) as He helps believers to be the example in speech, in life, in love, in faith, and in purity (1 Tim. 4:12).

Sample Speaking Topics: "Goal Setting", "Overcoming Rejection", "Building Godly & Healthy Relationships" "Walking in Wisdom" and more

Bibliography

Aland, Kurt. A History of Christianity. Philadelphia: Fortress Press, 1986.

Aland, Kurt. Synopsis of the Four Gospels. Stuttgart: Biblia-Druck, 1971.

Alexander, Patrick H. Dictionary of Pentecostal and Charismatic Movement (Grand Rapids Zondervan Publishing House, 1988) 770

Barth, Karl. Dogmatics in Outline. New York: Philosophical Literary, 1949.

Bartleman, Frank. Azusa Street. Plainfield, NJ: Logos International, 1980.

Bennett, Dennis. The Holy Spirit and You. Plainfield: Logos International, 1971.

Bennett, Rita and Dennis Bennett. The Holy Spirit and You. Plainfield: Logos International, 1971.

Beyerhans, Peter and Henry Lefever. The Responsible Church and the Foreign Mission. Grand Rapids: Eerdmans, 1964.

Bierderwolf, William E. A Help to the Study of the Holy Spirit. Grand Rapids: Zondervan Publishing House, 1936.

Bruce, F..F. Paul Apostle of the Heart Set Free. Grand Rapids: Eerdmans.

Bruner, Frederick D. The Doctrine and Experience of the Holy Spirit in the Pentecostal Movement and Correspondingly in the New Testament. Los Angeles: Frederick Dale Bruner, Hamburg, 1963.

Budgen, Victor. The Charismatics and the Word of God. Weslyn, Hertfordshire, England: Evangelical Press, 1985.

Chadwick, Samuel. The Way to Pentecost. 1932. Reprint. London, Sydney, Auckland, Toronto: Hodder and Stoughton, 1951.

Chandler, Dalton R. Tongues Life as of Fire. Springfield, MO: The Gospel Publishing House, 1945.

Christenson, Laurence. Speaking in Tongues and Its Significance for the Church. Minneapolis: Bethany House Publishers, 1968.

Clark, Otis and Williams, Gwen. The Azusa Mission. Bixby, OK. Holiness Mission Publishing 1993.

Conn, Charles W. A Balanced Church. Cleveland: Pathway Press, 1975.

Conn, Charles W. Like a Mighty Army—A History of the Church of God. Cleveland: Pathway Press, 1977.

Cox, Dr. Raymond L. The Four Square Gospel. Salem: Foursquare Publications, 1969.

Davis, Burnie. How to Have God's Miracle Power in Your Life. Tulsa, OK: Praise Books, 1982.

Dugas, Paul D. The Life and Writings of Elder G.T. Haywood. Cherokee: Apostolic, 1968.

Dunn, James. baptism in the Holy Spirit. The Westminster Press, 1970.

Earle, Ralph. Exploring the New Testament. Kansas City: Beacon Hill Press, 1955.

Erickson, Millard J. Christian Theology. Grand Rapids: Baker Book House.

Ervin, Howard. Conversion Initiation and the baptism In the Holy Spirit. Hendrickson Publishers, Inc., 1984.

Ervin Howard. Spirit baptism. Hendrickson Publishers, Inc., 1987.

Feene, P. Speaking With Tongues. Samuel Macauley Jackson.

Forbes, James. The Holy Spirit and Preaching. Nashville: Abingdon Press, 1989.

Gee, Donald. Pentecost. Springfield, MO: Gospel Publishing House, 1932.

Gee, Donald. The Pentecostal Movement. London: Elim, 1949.

Golder, Bishop Morris E., M.A. History of the Pentecostal Assemblies of the World. Indianapolis: Bishop Morris E. Golder, 1973.

Gordon, A. J. The Ministry of the Spirit. Minneapolis: Bethany House Publishers, 1985.

Grant, W.V. How to Receive the Holy Spirit baptism. Dallas: W.V. Grant, 1921.

Hagin, Kenneth E. Understanding The Anointing. Tulsa: Rhema Bible Church, 1983.

Heron, Alasdair I. C. The Holy Spirit in the Bible, the History of Christian Thought, and Recent Theology. Waco: Westminster Press, 1973.

Hibbert, Albert. The Secret of His Power. Tulsa, OK: Harrison House, 1982.

Hockins, Anthony. What About Tongue Speaking? Grand Rapids: Eerdmans, 1966.

Hull, Bill. The Disciple Making Pastor. Old Tappan: Fleming H. Revell Company, 1988.

Kane, J. Herbert. A Global View of Christian Missions. Grand Rapids: Baker Book House, 1971, 1975.

Kee, Howard. Understanding the New Testament. Englewood Cliff s, NJ: Prentice-Hall, Inc.

Ladd, George. The Theology of the New Testament. Grand Rapids: Eerdmans, 1974.

Lindsay, Gordon. Men Who Heard From Heaven. Garden City: The Voice of Healing Publishing Co., 1953.

McIntire, Carl. The Death of a Church. Collingswood: Christian Deacon Press, 1967.

McPherson, Aimee S. The Foursquare Gospel. Georgia Stiffler, Th.D.: Collaborator, 1946.

Metz, Donald S. Speaking in Tongues. Kansas City, MO: Nazarene Publishing House, 1964.

Mills, Watson E. Speaking in Tongues Let's Talk About It. Waco: Word Books, 1973.

Mills, Watson E. Speaking in Tongues. Grand Rapids: Eerdmans, 1986.

Myland, Rev. D. Wesley. The Latter Rain Covenant. Springfield, MO: Temple Press, 1910.

Nelson, Douglas J. For Such A Time As This (England: University of Birmingham, 1981) 45.

Nickel, Thomas R. Azusa Street Outpouring. Hanford: Great Commission International, 1956, 7.

O'Connor, Edward D. Pope Paul and the Spirit Charisms and Church Renewal in the Teaching of Paul VI. Notre Dame: Ave Maria Press, 1974.

Ortloff, Hazel. The Happiest People on Earth. Old Tappan: Fleming H. Revell Company, 1975.

Paris, Arthur E. Black Pentecostalism. Amherst: The University of Massachusetts Press, 1982.

The Pentecostal Holiness Church. The Pentecostal Message Number Two. Franklin Springs: The Publishing House Pentecostal Holiness Church, 1953.

Pentecostal Preachers. The Pentecostal Message. Franklin Springs, GA: The Publishing House Pentecostal Holiness Church, 1950.

Ross, German R. and Associates. History and the Formative Years of the Church of God in Christ. Memphis: Church of God in Christ Publishing House, 1969.

St. Basil The Great. On The Holy Spirit. Crestwood, NY: Athens Printing Company, 1980.

Samarin, William J. Tongues of Men and Angels. New York: Macmillan, 1972.

Sargent, William. Some Cultural Group Objective Techniques and Their Relation to Modern Treatment. London: Longman Green, 1949.

Schweizer, Eduard. The Holy Spirit.

Seven Assemblies of God Ministers. The Pentecostal Pulpit. Springfield, MO: Gospel Publishing House, 1964.

Snyder, Howard A. Liberating the Church. Downers Grove: Inter-Varsity Press, 1983.

Swete, Henry B. The Holy Spirit in the New Testament. London: Macmillan, 1909.

Szagg, Frank, Glenn Hinson and Wayne E. Oates. Glossalia. Nashville and New York: Abingdon Press, 1967.

Toussaint, Stanley D. First Corinthians Thirteen and the Tongues Question. Philadelphia: Presbyterian and Reformed, 1967.

Veteran Members. The Apostolic Faith. Portland: Headquarters, 1965.

Wagner, C. Peter. On the Crest of the Wave of Becoming a World Christian. Ventura: Regal Books, 1983.

Warfield, Benjamin. Miracles: Yesterday and Today. Grand Rapids: Eerdmans, 1953.

Wood, Leon. The Holy Spirit in the Old Testament. Grand Rapids: Zondervan, 1976.

Dissertations

Bosch, F.W. Archibald. "The Holy Spirit in the Light of the Teachings of Jesus and of Paul." Th.M. thesis, University School of Theology, 1940.

Bruner, Frederick D. "The Doctrine and Experience of the Holy Spirit in the Pentecostal Movement and Correspondingly in the New Testament." Apparatus to the diss., Ev. Theol. Faculty of the University of Hamburg: Hamburg, 1963.

Scotts, George R. "The History of the Modern Pentecostal Movement in France." M.A. diss., Texas Tech University, 1973.

Newspapers/Magazines

Corum, Fred T. "Tongues Like A Fire." 1981.

The Apostolic Faith, Volume I, No. 9, Los Angeles, CA, June to September 1907.

The Apostolic Faith, Volume I, No. 8, Los Angeles, CA, May 1907.

The Apostolic Faith, Volume I, No. 6, Los Angeles, CA, February to March, 1907.

The Apostolic Faith, Volume I, No. 11, Los Angeles, CA, October to January 1908.

The Apostolic Faith, Volume I, No. 5, Los Angeles, CA, January, 1907.

The Apostolic Faith, Volume I, No. 6, Los Angeles, CA February to March, 1907.

The Apostolic Faith, Volume I, No. 3, Los Angeles, CA, November, 1907.

The Apostolic Faith, Volume I, No. 1, Los Angeles, CA, September, 1906.

The Apostolic Faith, Volume I, No. 12, Los Angeles, CA, January, 1908.

The Apostolic Faith, Volume I, No. 4, Los Angeles, CA, December, 1906.

The Apostolic Faith, Volume I, No. 10, Los Angeles, CA, September, 1907.

Full Gospel Men's Voice, Volume IV, No. 9, Southern California, October, 1956.

"Azusa Street" Roots Series. Logos Magazine, September 1980.

"Spiritual Climate" New Wine, Los Angeles, CA, 1906.

"Azusa Street Mission" Pentecostal Evangel, Los Angeles, CA, April 12, 1981.

Synan, Vinson. "Azusa Street, The Roots of Revival." Logos Journal, March/April, 1981.

Nickels, Thomas R. "Azusa Street Outpouring." Hanford, CA: Great Commission International, 1956.

Message of the Apostolic Faith, Volume I, No. 1, April 1939.

Endnotes

Cover Pics: https://youtu.be/VPm980ATPa4,

http://comunidadesantarosa.com.br/2018/05/18/pentecostes-e-o-espirito-santo/

Preface: Mark Crow

Introduction: John Harker

1-William Turner, The Pentecostal Message (Franklin Springs: The Pentecostal Holiness Church, 1950), 53.

2-Turner, 53.

3-Turner, 53.

4-Vinson Synan, The Holiness Pentecostal Movement in the United States (Grand Rapids: William B. Eerdmans Publishing company, 1971) 35.

5-Synan, 35

6-Synan, 35.

7-Morris E. Golder, History of the Pentecostal Assemblies of the World, (Indianapolis: Golder, M.A., 1973) 8.

8-Golder, 10.

9-Golder, 10.

10-Golder, 10.

11-Golder, 10.

12-Fredrick Dale Bruner, The Doctrine and Experience Of The Holy Spirit In The Pentecostal Movement And Correspondingly In the New Testament (Los Angeles: Hamburg, 1963)

13-Morton, Kelsey, Tongue Speaking (New York: Crossroads, 1981) 73.

14-G.T. Haywood and Paul D. Dugas, The Life And Writings of G.T. Haywood (Stockton: Apostolic Press, 1968) 21.

15-Nelson, 45.

16-Nelson, 45.

17-Nelson, 45.

18-David W. Dorries, The Forgotten History of the Azusa Street Revival, Centering Upon the Life and Thought of William J. Seymour, Address to Interns Class, Higher Dimension Church, 10 June 1993, 3.

19-Dorries, 4.

20-Dorries, 4.

21-Nelson, 45.

22-Donald S. Metz, Speaking In Tongues (Kansas city: Nazarene Publishing House, 1964), 32.

23-Vinson Synan, "Azusa Street Revival", New Wine, September, 1980, Root Series, 1.

24-Synan, New Wine, 30.

25-Synan, New Wine, 30.

26-Klaude Kendrick, The Promise Fulfilled (Springfield: Gospel Publishing House), 37.

27-Golder, 18-19.

28-Golder, 18.

29-Vinson Synan, "Azusa Street: The Roots of Revival", Logos Journal, March-April, 1981, 10.

30-Dorries, 3.

31-Dorries, 3.

32-James S. Tinney, William Joseph Seymour: Father of Sixty Million Pentecostals, (Philadelphia: Annual Convention of the Association for the Study of Afro-American Life and History, 30-31, October 1981.) 3.

33-Brunner, 41.

34-Metz, 32.

35-Metz, 32.

36-Stanley Howard Frodsham, With Signs Following (Springfield: Gospel Publishing House, 1926), 20.

37-Metz, 33.

38-Metz, 33.

39-Metz, 33.

40-Alexander, 770.

41-Nelson, 58.

42-Tinney, 3.
43-Nelson, 67.
44-Alexander, 780.
45-Metz, 33-34.
46-Metz, 34.
47-Metz, 34.
48-Nelson, 59.
49-Emma Cotton, Message of the "Apostolic Faith, April, 1939, Vol. 1. No. 1, 1.
50-Cotton, 1.
51-Cliff, Full Gospel News, Vol. 4, No. 3, 2.
52-Cliff, 2.
53-Cliff, 2.
54-Cliff, 2.
55-Golder, 28
56-Cliff, 2.
57-Cliff, 2.
58-Vinson Synan, Azusa Street (South Plainfield: Logos International, 1980) 17.
59-Golder, 28
60-Nickel, 7.
61-Nickel, 6.
62-Nickel, 6.
63-Bartleman, 57-58.
64-Nelson, 12
65-Bartleman, 42.
66-Bartleman, 42.
67-Brunner, The Doctrine and Experience of the Holy Spirit in the Pentecostal Movement, 32.
68-Brunner, 32.
69-Brunner, 32.
70-Brunner, 32.
71-Victor Budgen, The Charismatics and the Word of God (England: Evangelical Press, 1985) 185.

72-Budgen, 184.
73-Budgen, 185.
74-Budgen, 185.
75-Budgen, 186.
76-Budgen, 186.
77-Budgen, 186.
78-Budgen, 187.
79-Budgen, 187.
80-Budgen, 187.
81-Budgen, 187.
82-"The Apostolic Faith", Like As Of Fire, California: February-March, 1907, Vol. 1 no. 6, 1.
83-"The Apostolic Faith", Feb-Mar., 1907. Vol. 1, No. 6, 1. 94
84-"The Apostolic Faith, Los Angeles: October 1906, Vol. 1 No. 2, 1.
85-"The Apostolic Faith", Vol. 1, No 6, February-March, 1907, 2.
86-"The Apostolic Faith", Vol. 1 No. 6, February-March, 1907, 2.
87-B.H. Iwrin, "The Apostolic Faith" Vol. 7 April 1907, 4.
88- A.H. Argue, "The Apostolic Faith", 4.
89-A.H. Argue "The Apostolic Faith", 4.
90-A.H. Argue, "The Apostolic Faith", 4.
91-German R. Ross, History and Formative Years of the Church God In Christ with From The Life And Works of Its founder-Bishop C.H. Mason (Memphis: C.O.G.I.C. Publishing, Memphis, 1969), 14.
92-Ross, 14.
93-Ross, 17.
94-Ross, 18.
95-Charles Parham, Letter "The Apostolic Faith", Los Angeles: September, 1906, Vol. 1 No. 1, 1.
96-Parham, 1.
97-Bartleman, 174.
98-Bartleman, 174.
99-Bartleman, 174-175.

100-Synan, Azusa Street, 19.

101-Synan, Azusa Street, 19.

102-Synan, Azusa Street, 19.

103-Bartleman, 28.

104-Bartleman, 28.

105-Robert Coleman Dalton, Tongues Life As Of Fire (The Gospel Publishing House, 1945), 11.

106-Dalton, 11.

107-Alexandar, 33

108-Vinson Synan, Under His Banner, (F.G.B.M.F.I).

109-Fredrick R. Brunner, The Doctrine And Experience of The Holy Spirit in the Pentecostal Movement and Correspondingly in the New Testament (Hamburg: University of Hamburg, 1963), 37.

110-Edward Schweizer, The Holy Spirit, 10-19.

111-Leon Wood, The Holy Spirit in The Old Testament (Grand Rapids: Zondervan, 1976), 42-43.

112-Wood, 19-20.

113-Kurt Aland, Synopsis of the Four Gospels (Stuttgart: Biblia-Druck, 1971), 110.

114-Karl Barth, Dogmatics in Outline (New York: Philosophical Literary, 1949), 95.

115-Dennis Bennett, The Holy Spirit and You (Plainfield: Logos International, 1971)

116-Henry B. Swete, The Holy Spirit in the New Testament (London: MacMillan, 1909) 130-135.

117-Donald Gee, The Pentecostal Movement (London: Elim Press, 1949), 10.

118-Brunner, 30.

119-Laurence Christenson, Speaking in Tongues and Its Significance for the Church (Minneapolis: Bethany House Publishers, 1968), 72-79.

120-Anthony Hockins, What About Tongue Speaking? (Grand Rapids: Eerdmans, 1966), 16.

121-Stanley D. Toussaint, First Corinthians Thirteen and the Tongues Question (Philadelphia; Presbyterian and Reformed, 1967), 118-129.

122-Benjamin Warfield, Miracles: Yesterday and Today (Grand Rapids: Eerdmans, 1953), 6.
123-P. Feene, Speaking with Tongues (Samuel Macauley Jackson), 9.
124-William Sargent, Some Cultural Group Objective Techniques and Their Relation to Modern Treatment (London Longman Green, 1949), 367.
125-William J. Samarin, Tongues of Men and Angels (New York: Macmillan, 1972), 4.
126-F.F. Bruce, Paul Apostle of the Heart Set Free (Grand Rapids: Eerdmans), 153.
127-Brunner, Appartus, 75.
128-Howard Ervin, Spirit Baptisms (Hendrickson Publishers, 1987), 58-59.
129-A.J. Gordon, The Ministry of the Spirit (Minneapolis: Bethany House Publishers, 1985) 45. 97
130-James Dunn, Baptism in the Holy Spirit (The Westminster Press, 1970), 51.
131-Gordon, 45.
132-George Ladd, A Theology of the New Testament (Grand Rapids: Eerdmans, 1974) 295.
133-Bruce, 207-208.
134-Ralph Earle, Exploring the New Testament (Kansas City: Beacon Hill Press, 1955) 227.
135-Michael J. Wilkins, Following The Master (Grand Rapids: Zondervan Publishing House, 1992), 118.
136-Wilkins, 118.
137-Howard Kee, Understanding the New Testament (Englewood Cliff s: Prentice-Hall, Inc), 186.
138-Albert Hibbert, The Secret of His Power (Tulsa: Harrison House, 1982) 53.
139-Arthur E. Paris, Black Pentecostalism (Amherst: The University of Massachusetts Press, 1982), 22.
140-Paris, 22.
141-Paris, 22.
142-W.V. Grant, How to Receive The Holy Spirit Baptism (Gospel Publishing House, 1962)55.
143-Dalton, 125.
144-Dalton, 125.

145-Edward D. O'Connor, C.S.C.., Pope Paul and the Spirit (Indiana: Ave Maria Press, 1978), 18.
146-O'Connor, 18.
147-O'Connor, 18.
148-Paris, 15.
149-Howard Ervin, Conversion Initiation and the Baptism In the Holy Spirit (Hendrickson Publishers, Inc. 1984), 7.
150-Paul Elbert, Essays on Apostolic Themes (Peabody: Hendrickson Publishers, 1985), 2.
151-Elbert, 2.
152-Thomas R. Nickels, Full Gospel Men's Voice, October, 1956, 5.
153-Elbert, 3.
154-Alsadair I.C. Heron, The Holy Spirit (Philadelphia: The Westminster Press, 1983), 130.
155-Heron, 130.
156-Heron, 131.
157-Heron, 131.
158-Charles W. Conn, Like A Mighty Army (Cleveland: Pathway Press, 1977), 7.
159-Conn, 7.
160-Conn, 29.
161-Heron, 131.
162-Dalton, 119.
163-Dalton, 119.
164-Dalton, 119-120.
165-Gordon Lindsay, Men Who Heard From God (Garden City: Voice of Healing Publishing, 1953), 2.
166-Nickels, Full Gospel, 10
167-Nickels, Full Gospel, 27
168-Nickels, Full Gospel, 28
169-Fredrick Dale Brunner, The Doctrine And Experience of the Holy Spirit in the Pentecostal Movement and Correspondingly in the New Testament (Hamburg: University of Hamburg, 1963), 1.

170-Synan, Azusa Street, 9.
171-Synan, Azusa Street, 9.
172-Synan Azusa Street, 9.
173-Synan, Azusa Street, 9.
174-Dalton, 116.
175-Clark/Williams, 55.
176-Alexander, 779.
177-Golder, 27.
178-Golder, 27.
179-Nelson, 12.
180-Clark/Williams, 87.
181-Clark/Williams, 69.
182-Clark/Williams, 184.
183-Alexander, 33.
184-Clark/Williams, 90.
185-Nickels, 11-26.
186-Nelson, 14.